RACIALLY
EQUITABLE
TEACHING

Dr. Margie Wiggins Jones

10/09

NAME

Denver, CO.

Rethinking Childhood

Joe L. Kincheloe and Gaile Cannella
General Editors

Vol. 40

PETER LANG
New York • Washington, D.C./Baltimore • Bern
Frankfurt am Main • Berlin • Brussels • Vienna • Oxford

Mary E. Earick

RACIALLY EQUITABLE TEACHING

Beyond the Whiteness of Professional Development for Early Childhood Educators

PETER LANG
New York • Washington, D.C./Baltimore • Bern
Frankfurt am Main • Berlin • Brussels • Vienna • Oxford

Library of Congress Cataloging-in-Publication Data

Earick, Mary E.
Racially equitable teaching: beyond the whiteness of professional development
for early childhood educators / Mary E. Earick.
p. cm. — (Rethinking childhood ; v. 40)
Includes bibliographical references and index.
1. Racism in education—United States. 2. Discrimination in education—United States.
3. Educational equalization—United States. 4. Early childhood education—
Political aspects—United States. I. Title. II. Series.
LC212.2.E27   372.1829—dc22   2008006255
ISBN 978-1-4331-0113-7 (hardcover)
ISBN 978-1-4331-0114-4 (paperback)
ISSN 1086-7155

Bibliographic information published by **Die Deutsche Bibliothek**.
Die Deutsche Bibliothek lists this publication in the "Deutsche
Nationalbibliografie"; detailed bibliographic data is available
on the Internet at http://dnb.ddb.de/.

Cover art by Mary E. Earick
Cover design by Sophie Boorsch Appel

The paper in this book meets the guidelines for permanence and durability
of the Committee on Production Guidelines for Book Longevity
of the Council of Library Resources.

© 2009 Peter Lang Publishing, Inc., New York
29 Broadway, 18th floor, New York, NY 10006
www.peterlang.com

Printed in the United States of America

• Contents •

• Figures, Photos, and Tables •

Figures

Photos

Tables

As a classroom teacher I prided myself on my social justice and equality focus. I believed sincerely that if I could support and deliver a curriculum that honored multiracial, multiethnic, and multilingual learners, my students would have tools to succeed in public education. I loved teaching. I loved greeting each of my students and watching as they took ownership of new knowledge. Each day was exciting and full of adventures. Yet after my sixteen years in the classroom, I realized that I was offering my students only a very limited education. I watched as young, intelligent, and creative students internalized racism and relegated themselves to various social statuses that were privileging Whites and disprivileging children of Color. What I became painfully aware of was my limited knowledge of the defining role race plays in how I self-identified and subsequently applied what I viewed as equity pedagogies. In addition, I realized the limited impact individual equity projects have when culturally schools are not aware of the need of addressing racial, ethnic, cultural and multilingual identity development. Structurally, the U.S. is focused on basic skills and moving toward national standards based on dominant beliefs in our society rather than multiple perspectives on what is important or communicated as official knowledge.

Early childhood teachers, educators, scholars, and policymakers have dedicated themselves to addressing gender equity and have made statistically significant progress in closing the achievement gap in science and mathematics. Gender equity has become an accepted canon of knowledge presented and discussed in our early childhood education programs and professional development projects. Today the achievement gap is decidedly race-based and in need of the same collective effort to affect systemic change as we have historically done in the area of gender equity. It is not only the disproportionate numbers of Hispanic[1] and Black[2] children who live in poverty based on their racial subgroups, but also Whites who comprise the largest number of children living in poverty (U.S. Bureau of the Census, 2004). This information makes clear that low socioeconomic status alone can no longer justify the racial nature of the achievement gap. Focusing on alternative theories and the extensive critical scholarship that has been conducted is necessary to close that gap.

When discussing critical issues of race with students, colleagues, and friends, emotions rise and conversations become heated unlike discussions revolving around gender and socioeconomics. For this reason, we each must be prepared to move out of our comfort zones and reflect on beliefs we overtly and covertly hold concerning race, just as we have done in the past with gender. Racially Equitable Teaching (RET) presents scholarship not typically read by early childhood teachers and educators, in an effort to support each of us as we strengthen our ability to build equitable classrooms.

Several terms I have used in the book need special definition in the context of RET. These terms are early childhood, educator, schooling, Whiteness, race, racism, and identity construction/deconstruction. Early childhood encompasses the period from the birth of a child through age eight. Children with a range of abilities and special needs as described by the National Association for the Education of Young Children are also part of this category. I separate the terms teacher and educator in the following manner: a teacher provides information and space within the classroom for discussion, which is needed to enter into a learning process, while an educator provides information, space, and encourages critique of the information presented on the basis of the lived experiences of the students. Although early childhood professionals can work in a variety of locations within a community, when discussing schooling, I will focus on Pre-K through grade three public urban inner city school programs. Schooling, the process of internalizing "the dominant meaning purveyed in formal curricula and school discourse" as presented by Levinson and Holland in *The Cultural Production of the Educated Person* (1996, p. 21), mediates the construction and deconstruction of group and perceived identities during this sensitive stage of early childhood. These identities are not biological or innate processes but socially mediated and therefore can be constructed of social norms or deconstructed based on those same norms. These sites of identity construction/deconstruction are places of struggle, struggle that students address on a daily basis as they apply agency. These sites of struggle reflect societal, political, and cultural battles. Weedon (1997) describes these sites of battle as "precarious, contradictory and in process, constantly being reconstituted in discourse each time we speak" (p. 106).

Although identities are interwoven and informed by each other, today by virtue of student outcomes in public education race matters in significant and tangible ways. When students struggle in schools they also struggle economically and socially when they leave schools, making race a form of capital. Race is a "social construction" (Omi & Winant, 1994, pp. 54-55; Weis, Fine, Weseen, & Wong, 2000, p. 39) that is "...[n]either an essence nor an illusion, it is an ongoing process of social and political struggle" (López, H., 1995, p. 193) that has "no genetic characteristics possessed by all members of any one group" (Ladson-Billings, 2000, p. 259). Racism is "a system of advantages based on race" (Lawrence & Tatum, 1997a, p. 7). This system of advantage is structural and manifests itself in Whiteness, defined by Allen (2001[3]) as "a system that bestows power and privilege on those who become identified as White and bestows disempowerment and disprivileges on those who become identified as People of Color."

• A C K N O W L E D G M E N T S •

T he transition from being a practitioner to an academic is difficult, but a necessary one to address structural change. Bridging theory and practice was critical to my work and the individuals who mentored me through that process were of the greatest importance. I was fortunate to have the guidance of Dr. Ricky Lee Allen throughout this transition. His understanding and commitment to issues of social justice transformed my thinking and inspired me to look for ways to use my practitioner identity as a conduit to my identity as a theorist. For this I will always be grateful. Dr. Mary Dudley consistently posed questions that made me pause and think deeply about my position. She also counseled on implications my work would have in the current educational times and in the future of early childhood education. Dr. Nancy Lopez's insightful reviews of my work strengthened my ability to move past traditional educational research paradigms and look at the complex relationships that exist between sociology, cognition, and education. Dr. Ruth Galvin-Trinidad gave me support and advice on how to effectively communicate my thoughts on paper, something I was rarely asked to do as a classroom teacher. Dr. Shirley Steinberg's work informed much of my theoretical lens as a kindergarten teacher. The mentorship and opportunities she and the staff at Peter Lang gave me focused my work and my future research. Rich Burness, Louise Golden, and Chris Hart-Rooney reviewed, edited, and constantly debated over how to present this material in a proactive and empowering model. It was and is their work and passion as early childhood educators that informed much of my own classroom pedagogies. The "Porch Ladies" have refined and clarified the need for critical scholarship inspiring me to continue my research in Racially Equitable Teaching. They are and will continue to be my critical friends. My husband Doug makes sure I never wander too far from the day-to-day realities encountered by students, families, administrators, and public education teachers. His insights augment my desire to succeed and work toward empowering educators to apply transformative antiracist pedagogies. He is a partner and collaborator in every aspect of my work. The dedication and generous gift of time from each of these individuals are reflected in this book.

CHAPTER I

Teaching and Racial Isolation

The social and political implications of the white habitus are very significant. The universe of whiteness navigated on an everyday basis by most whites fosters a high degree of homogeneity of racial views and even of the manners in which whites express these views. Despite the civil rights revolution, whites, young and old, live a fundamentally segregated life that has attitudinal, emotional, and political implications.   Bonilla-Silva (p. 125, 2003)

My undergraduate years were a sea of Whites. All my professors were White and I had only one classmate of Color in my early childhood certification program. Although many of us were to teach in urban schools we were racially isolated from colleagues of color, professors, and staff at my university, which professed to be an institution dedicated to multicultural ideals and practices. The absence of People of Color attending and teaching at our university was considered an outcome of low socioeconomics; it was never discussed from a race perspective. As Bonilla-Silva (2003) has argued and documented, this class-based belief assisted in normalizing our hypersegregation and isolation from People of Color, supporting a color-blind ideology. Alarmingly, there was a distinct belief that those of us who would teach in urban schools were of the highest moral fabric, willing to sacrifice personal time and energy beyond a traditional workday. This extra work was allegedly due to the fact that we would have to teach students with many deficits.

My racial isolation began when I entered first grade at Our Lady of Lourdes School in Queens, New York. My neighbors represented several countries, languages, and races, yet I never interacted with them socially or academically once I left the public school where I attended kindergarten. It was not until the early 1980s, when I lived and worked in New Haven, CT, at the age of twenty-two, that I began to deconstruct the relationship between my racial isolation and ideology and reconstruct a realist view of the structural inequities in our society that promote White supremacy. I came to realize that racial isolation is a process that begins in early childhood, is supported in our schools, and continues throughout our lives. Although I was racially isolated in my formal schooling, I was fortunate to have counter experiences as a neighborhood teacher in an educational community where families self-identified predominately as African American and Black in CT and through the patience of my stepfather, James, who is also African American. In addition, when I was in the military stationed in Europe, I enjoyed the freedom to socialize with the local residents. These same residents considered the majority of soldiers in my unit, predominantly People of Color, unintelligent and undesirable. Over time, these experiences gave me an understanding of the privileges I have as a White female. My friends of Color in the military explained to me that this happened on virtually every base, nationally and internationally. This communicated to me how racial isolation is not only a U.S. phenomenon, but also a global one. I have had far more opportunities to succeed academically and advance socially than my family, friends, colleagues, and neighbors of Color.

When I came to work as a kindergarten teacher in Connecticut, I had high hopes of enjoying the diversity of my neighborhood and of being a productive member within it as a teacher at our local school. When I arrived, only one teacher was not White and I was told that she was a troublemaker. Of the 4% of students were White, all were considered high performers whose morale was brought down by students of Color. You would hear the teachers comment, "What a shame if he [a White student] was only in a different school he would have a chance" and "She [a White student] is losing all her ambition to succeed here." African Americans males were the majority of students in self-contained special education classes, and there was an air of oppression in the building. I was told that our students were in need of highly structured environments; they had to overcome the lack of structure and educational opportunities in their homes. My principal instructed me to "run a tight ship," that is, my twenty-eight kindergarten students were expected to walk quietly in lines, work quietly in class, eat quietly in the lunchroom, and never talk back or question the instructions from teachers and administrators; if accomplished, they would be awarded twenty minutes of recess. These types of incidents not only contribute to a lack of belief by teachers that urban students have a capacity to learn and excel (Delpit, 1995; Kohn, 1998; Perry, 2002; Steele, 2003; Suarez-Orozco, 2002; Valdez, 1996), but also lead them to blame students of Color for their lack of motivation and for hindering the achievement of White students.

I already knew of these conditions in schools before my first full time teaching assignment. Prior to my kindergarten appointment, I worked as a substitute teacher for four years in a number of schools in Connecticut. As a substitute teacher and parent, I witnessed kindergartens where students talked quietly while moving through hallways, were encouraged to ask questions and look for alternative solutions while doing class work, were chatting, and moving freely between lunch and outdoor areas, and where time outside the walls of the classroom was considered a valuable learning environment, not a reward for docility. For some reason these schools were disproportionately White in a city where 89% (CT Department of Education, 2006) of students were People of Color. The methods I was being instructed to apply in my kindergarten were not the methods applied in the predominantly White, high-performing schools overtly perpetuating racialized differentiations through the pedagogies applied by early childhood teachers in our district.

I have found that the racial inequities I observed in Connecticut were not unique. Since 1985, I have been employed by both early childhood schools and educational institutions and have seen similar patterns in my work as an educator, staff developer, and mentor in New Mexico, South Carolina, and California. This has prompted me to look at structural issues in education causing this behavior in White teachers. I also came to realize that the education of our children has become dependent on the perceived needs of the global economy, driven by a neoliberal discourse that works towards creating a myth that transnational capital is a common global interest to mask the overprivileging of Whites. This allows for an educational system based on commodities and marketing strategies that are supported through the standardized academic goals and testing. To compete and retain their position of dominate global power, the U.S. views students as consumers and teachers as managers, each dependent upon the market-based needs to ensure future economic success. Lipman (2004) synthesizes post-9/11 neoliberal globalization discourse and its relationship to education when she states,

> The importance of the symbolic dimensions of this conservative assault cannot be underestimated (see Bourdieu, 1998). But a crucial aspect of this process is also social practices in everyday life that render people docile, obedient, and easily manipulated and conforming (Foucault, 1971). In this context, I argue that we need to rethink the meanings of dominant education policies grounded in accountability and centralized regulation of schools (p55).

In other words, the future of our children is market-driven by the U.S. economic agenda, which exerts power and politics over their lives. This rhetoric supports the U.S. government's use of neoliberal, rather than critical, discourse to explain the achievement gap between Whites and People of Color as a matter of individual choice, separating the individual from the social structures that currently and historically reproduce the color line (Du Bois, 1903) in our schools.

So rather than thinking about issues of social justice while in schools, students are bombarded with the No Child Left Behind (NCLB) mandates for national standards and accountability in the name of perceived equity. This new form of student surveillance succeeds in focusing national attention on individual opportunity rather than social opportunity and has dire outcomes. When we examine who prospers financially and socially from our educational system, it is, without doubt, the Whites. Whites consistently outperform People of Color on standard measures of success. These tests historically and currently are used to track students, as early as preschool, as high performers or low performers, directly impacting developing identities. This system of tracking in education is then the pipeline to higher education, leading to increased social and economic advantages, making Whiteness a form of human capital. Therefore, Whiteness, as an economic and social asset, promotes a racial hierarchy that privileges Whites over all others, sustaining a society grounded in White supremacy that functions predominantly through the sweat equity of workers of Color and their embodiment of subservient identities. These workers were, are, and will be our children of Color, and their educational managers are and will be overwhelmingly White teachers.

National surveys (NCES, 2004) report that 90% of elementary school teachers and 60% of students are White. These teachers have had limited to no experience with individuals outside of their own race (Bonilla-Silva, 2003; Gay, 1993) prior to teaching in the public schools. Teachers in urban schools typically have a disproportionate number of students of Color. By fourth grade only 5% of White students are in high-poverty schools (NCES, 2004). These schools, serving large numbers of low socioeconomic status students of Color, have larger class sizes, and fewer teachers and counselors. They also have fewer and inferior academic courses, extracurricular activities, books, materials, supplies, computers, libraries, and special services (Darling-Hammond, 2004). Therefore our urban students have limited educational materials, poor access to information, and are predominantly taught by White teachers. If White teachers believe the 5% of White students in their high-poverty schools are high performers "brought down" by the students of Color, as my colleagues in Connecticut did, then what hope do we offer the 95% of students of Color who are then the "Others," those who are perceived as having deficits?

Conversations with White teachers in early childhood urban schools in Connecticut, South Carolina, New Mexico, and California have illuminated to me their tendencies to accept racial problems as belonging to the Other rather than critically reflect on the root of the issue or problem (Frankenberg, 1993), or to blame the victim while ignoring their role as perpetrator (Kailin, 1999) in racial conflicts. Teachers distinguish the Other and shift the "blame" of racial problems by focusing on the individual as being in control of his or her destiny rather than by group associations. This process negates the structural aspects of racism in society, promoting color blindness and racial isolation.

While I lived in Connecticut, I heard many young White teachers, who had moved there to teach, extol the wonderful diversity of the city. They even claimed to support political organizations that promoted urban renewal, equitable housing, and high-quality education. Yet, when their own children grew to school-going age, they either sent them to private schools or moved to nearby suburbs. When I asked my colleagues why they moved, they would say, "The poverty is getting worse and the kids are too needy," "The city is too hectic," or "I don't feel safe anymore." They said this at a time when the poverty and crime rates were decreasing, and it was these same White families who used all the museums, arts programs, fairs, parks, and shopping areas on a daily basis. I saw these fellow White teachers as much after they left the city as when they were my neighbors. The difference was that they now packed themselves up in cars and went home to all-White neighborhoods and all-White schools and routinely commented on how much they missed the diversity of living in the city. They never mentioned race as a reason for moving; in fact, they consciously worked toward ignoring it, saying, "I don't want to be viewed as racist, it's the poverty, I love working with these kids [in the city]," and "my kids deserve to feel safe." This White talk (McIntyre, 1997) is a major tenet of a color-blind ideology, and their action of moving to racially isolated neighborhoods communicates unconscious beliefs about race. They indicate to society and their children that White neighborhoods and White schools are smarter, calmer, and safer. I taught for two years in an affluent, most sought-after suburban White school in Connecticut and did not experience a significant difference in school culture and climate.

The racial isolation geographically and professionally exhibited by my White colleagues is one example of how early childhood teachers promote Whites as the criterion group in education through the creation of norms. It was normal for the Whites to be high performers and students of Color to be low performers. It was normal for teachers and parents of Color, who voiced concerns over racism, to be ostracized and labeled troublemakers, and it was normal for the majority of White teachers to leave work and drive to White suburbs. In education, teachers view Whiteness as normal and typical, and it has become a standard for what is right, good, and true (McIntyre, 1997), creating and fixing the norms we assess our students by. These norms then inform our racial ideologies that we make visible in our teaching through the application of pedagogies and the artifacts in our classrooms.

Antiracist scholars and organizations have a long history of moving White early childhood teachers from a color-blind ideology to a racial realism. The National Association for the Education of Young Children published the *Anti-Biased Curriculum: Tools for Empowering Young* (Derman-Sparks) in 1989. It was the first book I used as a kindergarten teacher in order to learn how to bring race into classroom discussions. Rethinking Schools, the Southern Poverty Law Center (SPLC), Teaching for Change, and the Network for Educators on the Americas (NECA) have, and continue to add, publications and tools to a growing body of antiracist materials teachers can apply in their classrooms. Internationally, the newly formed Diversity in Early Childhood Education and Training (DECET) is networking resources and groups throughout Europe. Each of these organizations is an example of the deep commitment of antiracist educators to create equitable educational communities to achieve social justice in early childhood education. But as antiracist educator and advocate Troyna argues in "A New Planet? Tackling Racial Inequality in All-White Schools and Universities" (1989), antiracist education should not only discuss racism but also investigate how to transform schools into action-based centers for social justice. Nieto (2002) has recently reaffirmed this argument when she stated, "antiracist professional development pays insufficient attention to successful change strategies" (p. 67). Historically, U.S. antiracist professional development has focused on personal narratives (Landsman, 2001; McIntosh, 1992; Paley, 2000), race consciousness (McIntyre, 1997; Tatum & Brown, 2000a, 200b; Zeichner, 1996), and teacher perceptions (Kailin, 1999; Ladson-Billings, 2000, 2001) without documenting observable changes in the classrooms.

Recently, Obidah and Teel (2001) grounded their work in classroom observations through "teacher to teacher collaboration across race and culture" (p. 2). Within this relationship a White teacher/researcher was mentored and coached by a Black teacher/researcher over three years to "help White teachers—as well as all middle-class teachers to overcome 'cross-cultural disorientation'" (p. 104). They recommend that this process should be "incorporated into teacher education programs that train teachers for urban schools and into staff development in urban schools" (p. 104). Working directly in classrooms represents a new movement in antiracist professional development. Its importance cannot be disputed, but my question is whether it is realistic to have teachers of color mentor all-White urban teachers when they are outnumbered nine to one in the U.S. And what responsibility do White professors in higher education have in this process of cross-cultural disorientation?

Although the findings in personal narratives, race consciousness, White teacher perceptions, and (with limited study) teacher-to-teacher mentorship have assisted in justifying the need to address race and racism in classrooms, observable changes in teaching strategies across multiple classrooms is an area of antiracist education in which I see opportunities for growth. The development and application of transformative pedagogies or change strategies hold the potential to create tools that White teachers can use to combat institutional racism. But they cannot be implemented or documented until White teachers accept, understand, and identify the racial ideologies they practice and make visible in their classrooms daily. Identification of ideology moves teacher reflection from a passive act to a transformative one through the application of antiracist change strategies. The pivotal role of ideology in educational transformation is presented in Leonardo's book *Ideology, Discourse and School Reform* (2003). Leonardo spent a full year with two fellow researchers observing an inquiry group made up of nine teachers, two administrators, and two district officers, in an urban middle school. A key outcome of his analysis was directed toward teacher empowerment for change and social justice. Leonardo states, "If teacher reflection is going to be empowering, then it must extend beyond its sloganeer status and approach the contours of ideological reflection" (p. 236), identifying ideology as a critical component of transforming educational settings.

So how can teachers from racially isolated educational and social backgrounds know the needs of students and families of Color if they have not interacted with them? How do teachers know what a good school is? Or is it simply that White teachers associate good schools with White students and avoid reflecting on their own racial ideologies and how these ideologies impact classrooms? And, finally, how can teachers ensure that their students benefit from antiracist professional development? To answer such questions, I propose an anti-White supremacist theoretical framework called Racially Equitable Teaching (RET). I will do so through an ideological critique of professional development, White racial ideology, and racial projects currently in public early childhood educational programs. In addition, I will present an anti-White supremacist professional development project called Early Childhood Racial Identity Equity (ECRIE) as one method of addressing the need for White teachers to understand the reality of racial ideologies, how their racial ideologies impact student racial identities, and how they can apply RET. My intention is to assist White teachers as they identify strategies for transforming their racial ideologies and classroom pedagogies to work towards truly leaving no child behind.

If we are dedicated to closing the achievement gap, we must gain insights into how the current paradigms of professional develoment for teachers are organized around White racial ideology, and in what ways these paradigms embody types of White racial projects found in the U.S. My intention is to advance change in early childhood classrooms that will close the achievement gap between White and students of Color through critical reflection on the processes inhibiting and promoting racial ideology identification and RET by White educators. In addition, I will explore the root assumptions that would guide a truly anti-White supremacist professional develoment project. What would be some of the major concepts as well as concrete details? What would be the goals of this type of professional development? And how would you evaluate it?

Early childhood teachers and educators are not mandated in state certification systems to critically reflect on their group and individual ideologies, racial or otherwise, in preservice programs, which I view as an area in need of change. As I stated earlier, the work that has been done in the field of White teacher racial ideology has concentrated primarily on three areas: personal narratives, race consciousness, and teacher perceptions. Although this research offers important insights into the mechanisms Whites use to perpetuate their supremacy, it has yet to investigate three important questions: How are current paradigms of professional develoment for teachers organized around

White racial ideology? In what ways do these parardigms embody types of White racial projects found in the U.S.? And what root assumptions would guide a truly anti-White supremacist professional develoment project? Research on race consciousness and teacher perception only report on what the teachers say, which can be a learned behavior in a color-blind society that professes to be egalitarian with equal opportunity. What we say and what we do are separate but related actions. Perceptions are a component of ideology, having conscious and unconscious elements that shape and mediate our racial ideology. Communicating perceptions takes on conscious aspects—what we say—and unconscious aspects—what we do. It is in the analysis of this dichotomy that we can begin critical group-reflection and self-reflection on what it means to be a White teacher in a society that privileges White students.

My intention is to contribute to the fields of antiracist professional development, early childhood education, Whiteness studies, and ideological critique. It is my intention to work toward empowering teachers to take ownership of their classroom practices through critical reflection, documentation of artifacts, and implementation of transformative action in an effort to promote RET. I believe that White teachers can begin a process of knowledge production and ownership to emancipate themselves from the racist practices embedded in our educational system that supports White supremacy in the U.S. through racially equitable professional development. In addition, I wish to inform scholars and policymakers of the need to critically examine the racial nature of the achievement gap, how it is perpetuated through White professional development projects, and how it can be transformed through their support of RET professional development projects. In this manner we can promote an egalitarian society.

CHAPTER 2

Ideology, Race, and Education

Our public educational system supports White power and privilege that manifests itself in White supremacy. This is accomplished through the reproduction of White racial ideologies in our schools and best exemplified by the widely publicized achievement gap. Scholars in the field of critical race theory have identified prominent racial ideologies and structures that support specific racial projects driving U.S. policy, which I will present shortly. I intend to build on—in theory in the fields of ideology and race—what has been qualitatively and empirically documented in education and explain the need to envision a new theoretical framework for teaching, that of racial equity. This chapter serves as the foundation for RET, theoretically and practically.

In the first section of this chapter, I explore the connection between ideology and critical race theory, specifically looking at how racial ideologies are used as tools to maintain the overempowerment and privilege of Whites. In the second section, I show, through a discussion of how students have fared traditionally in U.S. public urban schools, how race is the decisive indicator as to whom we privilege in education. My conclusion calls for the awareness of the presence of race and explicates how White early childhood teachers could begin the process of emancipation from racist ideologies. This process is needed to bring us to the consciousness of how our roles as classroom teachers can perpetuate White supremacist educational practices and to apply transformative pedagogies in classrooms that support RET for all students.

Ideology and Critical Race Theory

I present ideology as nonessentialist, not placing it solely in the realm of the conscious as seen in Marxism or unconscious as presented by Marcuse and Althusser, but as multidimensional and moldable. Althusser (1971) argues that Ideological State Apparatuses (ISAs)—institutions such as education— instill in us values, desires, and preferences through ideological practice, which deem individuals and groups as subjects influenced by social contexts. Central to Althusser's theory of ideology is a shift from the subject as a self-conscious agent to a product of society. Although the role of ISAs in the formation of dominant ideologies is critical, the role of agency in transforming our dominant ideologies is equally important. For these reasons, I ground my definition of ideology in the work of Giroux and Eagleton.

Giroux (2001) defines ideology as "the production, consumption and representation of ideas which can either distort or illuminate behavior" (p. 143) that has positive and negative moments. These positive and negative moments either promote social action or become hegemonic. Equally important to the definition is the location of one's behavior. Giroux argues that "human behavior is rooted in a complex nexus of structured needs, common sense, and critical consciousness, and that ideology is located in all of these aspects of human behavior and thought so as to produce multiple subjectivities and perceptions of the world and everyday life" (p. 146). He builds on Italian political theorist Gramsci's notion of ideology as a hegemonic process; however, he critiques Gramsci's view that this process is achieved through the consent of individuals and groups, recognizing that ideology "promotes human agency but at the same time exerts force over individuals and groups" (p. 145), through the "weight" ideology "assumes in dominant discourses, selected forms of socio-historical knowledge, specific social relations, and concrete material practices" (p. 145). This is a critical point because it allows for structural change in society through the identification of the processes and artifacts that promote hegemony. If we can shift the weight associated with hegemonic ideologies through counterideologies, then the possibility for transformation exists.

Equally important in the discussion of ideology is Eagleton's (1991) assertion that ideology is not simply theory but sets of beliefs that impact our daily lives by possessing the power to control nondominant peoples. To Eagleton, ideology is composed of "ideas and beliefs which help to legitimate the interests of a ruling group or class specifically by distortion and dissimulation" (p. 30). This allows for the manifestation and identification of dominant ideologies in the everyday workings of a given society. One method of identifying dominant ideologies is to examine social systems such as education. In public education, White, heterosexual, Eurocentric curriculum distorts the reality of the lived experiences of People of Color in the U.S. (Banks, 1993; Barba, Pang, & Tran, 1992; Janzen, 1994; McIntosh, 2000; Rist, 1991) and projects White power and privilege as natural outcomes of meritocracy and capitalism, thus justifying the racial nature of the achievement gap. This dominant ideology has created a false reality in education that is based on the perception that low-performing students are not hardworking and are maladjusted because of low socioeconomic status. Poverty rates for children are widely publicized and used to support this rhetoric. Educators will say that it is common knowledge that the majority of children living in poverty are Black followed by Hispanic/Latino. Indigenous Peoples of the Americas are typically invisible to educators. Policymakers use these statistics to support initiatives such as NCLB, laden with intervention models of education aimed at addressing perceived deficits. If we critically examine the poverty statistics, we see a different reality.

Table 1: Children Under Eighteen Living in Poverty by Race, 2006 [1]

Category	Number	Percent
All children under eighteen	13,286,000	17
White only, non-Hispanic	4,507,000	10
Hispanic or Latino	4,112,000	27
Black or African American	3,776,000	33
Asian	358,000	12
American Indian	229,000	33

If we look at the number of children living in poverty (see Table 1), we find that the majority are White, closely followed by Hispanic or Latino and Black or African American. The percent of children living in poverty is based on the total number of children in their racial subgroup, not actual numbers correlated with the total number of children in poverty. We see that a disproportionate number of Hispanic or Latino, Black or African American and Native American children live in poverty and Whites comprise the largest number of children living in poverty. If in fact economic status is the major cause of the low performance in schools, Whites should represent the lowest performance rates in public schools; yet they consistently outperform People of Color on standard measures of success. On the basis of this information, we can observe that low socioeconomic status no longer can account for the racial nature of the achievement gap, and that it is a distortion of reality used by the dominant ideology to justify their overempowerment and privilege in U.S. society. This leads us to the realization that race is in the everyday workings of our belief systems and therefore a central component of ideology.

For critical race theorists, realities such as this have been shaped over time by a series of "social, political, cultural, economic, ethnic, and gender factors and then crystallized into a series of structures that are now inappropriately taken as 'real'" (Guba & Lincoln, 1994, p. 110). Therefore, history and its

---

[1] Data source: Kids Count Data Center http://www.kidscount.org/datacenter/

context are meaningful and rich methodological tools to gain insights and understand the structural components of social inequities. Critical race theory is composed of two strands: equity and democracy. These strands encompass the values, ethics, and beliefs of both individuals and society. In other words, the ideologies held by dominant racial groups translate into whether a society is rooted in equity and democracy. As I exemplified with the current poverty rates of children in the U.S., our educational system distorts data to support a perceived class-based, rather than critical, argument for the achievement gap; this is an effort to justify the overrepresentation of Whites in high-performing schools. This support of the status quo, rather than equity and democracy, is a clear example of why a critical perspective on race is needed in society.

Critical race theory, as Lopez (2001) states, "abandons the neutral concept of a color-blind society in favor of a critical perspective that recognizes the normality and thus invisibility of racism in our daily lives" (p. 30). This promotes a society that understands the permanence of racism, what Bell (1992) terms a "racial reality." I use a critical race lens because the racial reality of early childhood students is one of indoctrination that spreads into notions of a meritocracy through a racialized teacher work force and an educational testing system that privileges Whites over all other peoples. This indoctrination process supports what Hill Collins (2000) terms a "matrix of domination" framework. Within this matrix, wealthy, heterosexual White males are at the top, owning the most power and privilege, and poor, lesbian, third world Black females are at the bottom, owning the least power and privilege. All others fall within this hierarchical matrix in descending order based on perceived racial identity, and thereafter on gender, sexual, and class identities by those of a socially constructed higher status.

In schools this allows for a standards-driven model on the basis of a White criterion group (Blau, 2003, p.1) that privileges White students. Giroux (1995) views this process of schooling as stressing "the primacy of choice over community, competition over cooperation, and (perceived) excellence over equity" (pp. ix-xi), or what Freire (1970) terms a "banking model of education" (p. 2). This ideology supports racial stratification systems historically and currently in place in the U.S. Race is a salient component of ideology because it is a visible aspect of ourselves that we present to society. Gender, sex, and language can be hidden in our society, if one chooses to do so, but race is permanent and public, playing a defining role in our daily lives.

Racial Ideology

Prominent racial ideologies include color-blind racism, Whiteness as property, the Other, legitimizing invisibility, and racial realism. These ideologies bridge the conscious and unconscious aspects of race in our society. A strong point of critical race theorists who study and present racial ideology is their attention to the relationship between sociocultural-political contexts and real outcomes for raced peoples. Rather than focusing on a perceived utopian or humanistic system of beliefs, they critique and illuminate the racist reality of our society, giving us counternarratives to the distorted White supremacist ideologies that have become commonsense notions of reality.

Color-Blind Racism

Grounded in structuralism, Bonilla-Silva builds on Omi and Winant's (1986) (concept of "racialized societies," categorizing actors as those who are beneficiaries or subordinates in racialized social systems1 (2001, pp. 11-12). He presents the case in White Supremacy and Racism (2001) and Racism without Racists (2003) that our racialized social system preserves White supremacy through the racially based frameworks he terms racial ideologies. According to him, color-blind racism is a post–civil rights ideology.

He defines color-blind racism as an ideology that "explains the contemporary racial inequality as the outcome of nonracial dynamics," allowing Whites to "rationalize minorities' contemporary status as the product of market dynamics, naturally occurring phenomena and blacks' imputed cultural limitation" (2003, p.2). Therefore, Whites perceive accepted racial norms as being of nonracial origins, allowing them to justify their position of power and privilege based on perceived moral deficits in People of Color and lower socioeconomic class Whites. And, as we will see, this belief in moral deficits found in color-blind ideology is a result of social and property rights gained by Whites through the Constitution. In effect, color blindness is not what one says but what one does.

Whiteness as Property

Legal scholar Cheryl Harris (1995) deconstructs the relationship between race and property rights that have supported dominant and subordinate roles in US society, through the racialization of identity. She states, "The racialization of identity and the racial subordination of blacks and Native Americans provided the ideological basis for slavery and conquest" (p. 277). It was this domination of People of Color that promoted the legislation of property

rights in the U.S. to ensure that Whites were racially and economically superior.

Language surrounding this dominant and subordinate relationship has
shifted over the years from "slave" and "free" to "Black" and "White" (p. 278)
and more recently from "underprivileged" and "privileged" to "at risk" or "tar-
get population" and "high achieving," in an effort to mask the reality of race
in society. Yet one only needs to examine our laws to see that Whites legis-
lated to dominate, and the ramifications of those laws are the lived experience
of all Americans today. Therefore, if our legal rights represent liberty and justice, what is good and true and righteous in the U.S., they also constitute a
system of beliefs that is racially motivated and maintained.

This ideology of Whiteness as property is grounded in material rights that
have become accepted social norms. Harris explains how the ideology came to
be invisible:

> Materially, these advantages became institutionalized privileges: ideologically, they
> became part of the settled expectations of whites—a product of the unalterable
> original bargain. The law masks as natural what is chosen; it obscures the
> consequences of social selection as inevitable. The result is that the distortions in
> social relations are immunized from truly effective intervention, because the existing
> inequities are obscured and rendered nearly invisible. (p. 287)

To change the historical and current ramifications of Whiteness as property, the legal system must initiate and support legislation, such as affirmative
action, to counter the belief that property is "the right to prohibit infringe-
ment on settled expectation, ignoring countervailing equitable claims predi-
cated on the right to inclusion" (p. 290).

The "Other"

As we have seen with the ideologies of color-blind racism and Whiteness
as property, subordination of People of Color has been sustained by social
norms rationalized through stereotypes embedded in belief systems. These
beliefs give the appearance of being "logical and natural," resulting in what
Crenshaw, Gotanda, Peller, and Thomas (1995) call legitimating ideology. The
structure, in place and supported through legitimating ideology, has created a
hierarchy in which the "existence of a clearly subordinated other group is con-
trasted with the norm in a way that reinforces identification with the dominant group" (p. 112). This dichotomy empowers those perceived as the
dominant group to avoid being identified with the Other, constituting a less
than human status. Fanon identified in *Black Skins, White Masks* (1967) the
fear based on skin color and race embedded in Western thought that creates

this Other. He explains how we only need to look at metaphors embedded in our language to illuminate the concrete and/or symbolic aspects of racism:

> The black man stands for the bad side of the character blackness, darkness, shadow, shades, night, the labyrinths of the earth, abysmal depths, blacken someone's reputation; and on the other side, the bright look of innocence, the white dove of peace, magical, heavenly light. (p. 189)

Crenshaw et al. present a legal case of how legitimating ideology uses the Other to promote racism. They argue that "Racism helps to create an illusion of unity through the oppositional force of a symbolic "other" creating a bond, a burgeoning common identity of nonstigmatized parties—whose identity and interests are defined in opposition to the other" (pp. 112-113). Laws awarded social and property rights to Whites, creating structural racism and the need for the symbolic Other.

Legitimizing Invisibility

Land acquisition in the U.S. was based on the right of explorers to colonize and conquer, and thus legitimize the extermination of Indigenous Peoples of the Americas. On South Carolina's <u>Sciway</u> Web page it reads that the Congaree Indians are "extinct." Yet it is documented on the same Web page that at least half of the Congaree Indians who survived a smallpox epidemic in 1698 were taken as slaves in 1716 by the European settlers in Columbia and Charleston after the Yemassee War of 1715. It is more than possible that these people gave birth to children in South Carolina, calling into question the use of the word extinct. Congaree National Park mentions only the Congaree Indians' smallpox deaths on a timeline. Both groups relegate these first peoples of South Carolina as invisible Others. Sciway accomplishes this through the use of the term extinct and the Congaree National Park through exclusion. South Carolina is by no means unique in its legitimization of invisibility of Indigenous Peoples of the Americas. In fact, it one of the thirteen states that allows for state recognition of tribes to self-govern.

The U.S. mandates that Indigenous Peoples of the Americas, whom they identify as Native peoples, can be recognized by the federal government only if they meet the criteria that include "The petitioner has maintained political influence or authority over its members as an autonomous entity from historical times until the present" (25 CRF Part 83-b). As we can see with the Congaree Indians, 25 CRF Part 83-b would be impossible to accomplish since the surviving peoples were enslaved. As these laws legitimize invisibility, they allow society to do the same. Ruth Frankenberg (1993) studied forty White women across the U.S. and found that "racist discourse frequently accords a hyper visibility to African Americans and a relative invisibility to Asian Americans and Native Americans" (p. 12). For Blacks and African Americans in the U.S. the one-drop rule provided a level of visibility not applied to Indigenous Peoples of the Americas, since their existence was and is based on petition.

Racial Realism

Idealist ideologies include capitalism and the American Dream. Each is an example of legitimating ideologies as presented by Crenshaw et al. that are dependent upon the Other to justify the subordination of peoples in the U.S. Each creates and supports the myth that hard work will result in economic and social rewards, when in reality each is based on extracted labor resulting in commodity marketing that rewards a small dominant population. Social realism developed to counter idealism, which was viewed as a study of abstractions leading to false consciousness. Realists focused on what they saw and recorded these artifacts in a dispassionate manner, critiquing dominant ideology.

Legal realists challenged the traditional law structure to reform legislation toward a more equitable and just society (Bell, 1995, pp. 302-304). This was done by focusing on logic as applied to rights theory and its precedent. Bell holds that because racial equality is not possible, there is a need to narrow the field of realisms to racial realism to support equitable and just legal and social efforts. Adopting this ideology acknowledges the need for a "mechanism to make life bearable in a society where blacks are a permanent, subordinate class" (p. 307).

Bell identifies the logic of racial realism when he argues that

> Casting off the burden of equality ideology will lift the sights, providing a bird-eye view of situations that are distorted by race. From this broadened perspective on events and problems, we can better appreciate and cope with racial subordination. (p. 308)

Although Bell originally presented racial realism as a Black project, this logic has applications for all groups in the U.S. subordinate to Whites since the reality for all People of Color is that they were, and are, subject to White supremacy. With this in mind, I present racial realism as an ideology that can deconstruct structural racism by exposing color-blind racism, Whiteness as property, Othering, and legitimizing invisibility.

Racial Structures

To perpetuate these racial ideologies, society uses theoretical structures that allow for the distortion or illumination of social behaviors. Three prominent structures are hegemony, racial formation, and White supremacy. These structures mark a movement toward reenvisioning race as a central component to ideology, legitimizing race as the framework of privilege and power, and moving it into the realm of reality rather than perception.

Hegemony

Gramsci presented his theory of hegemony, which recognized the importance of ideology, human agency, and culture in society, in an effort to eliminate economic determinism from Marxism and present a more dialectic theory to explain how society is ruled and organized. Four major tenets of hegemony are as follows:

1. A dominant group succeeds in gaining consent from the masses to accept their moral, political, and cultural values and to follow their leadership;
2. Methods of gaining consent can include physical force, coercion, intellectual, moral, and cultural enticements;
3. Social and class struggles often serve as the catalyst of new hegemonic relationships and serve to shape ideas and beliefs of society;
4. Dominant ideology becomes "common sense" and widely accepted.

Hegemony was presented as "the practices of a capitalist class or its representatives to gain state power and maintain it later" (Simon, 1982, p. 23). Hegemony to Gramsci was the infusion of a system of values, attitudes, beliefs, and morality throughout a society, supporting a status quo in power relations. Hegemony thus becomes an "organizing principle" disseminated in everyday life through a socializing process that is a combination of coercion and consent. This results in the creation of "common sense" notions of reality that benefit the dominant group, normalizing their privileged place in society. Gramsci advanced Marx's notion of superstructures by categorizing them as those overtly coercive and those that were not. Overtly coercive superstructures were what he called the state or political society, predominately public institutions such as the government, police, armed forces, and the legal system. Noncoercive superstructures or civil society included churches, trade unions, political parties, cultural associations, clubs, and families. Although schools were originally categorized as noncoercive, with NCLB and the promotion of national standards and testing we can argue that public education today is overtly coercive.

It is important to note that to Gramsci, a Marxist, society had three inter-related components: production, the state, and the civil societies. Therefore, hegemony was originally grounded in a class argument that explains the domination of the masses as a result of their own consent. He believed that to change society from capitalism to socialism, an elite group of revolutionaries, which he referred to as intellectuals, had to create a counterhegemony for the masses. He discussed two types of intellectuals: traditional and organic. Traditional intellectuals were those individuals who viewed themselves as autonomous from dominant society; they included clergy and academics. Organic intellectuals emerged from the working class, were indoctrinated into the dominant system, and assisted in keeping the status quo until they shifted their ideological beliefs to counterhegemony. Gramsci advocated agency and discussed the need for alliances between traditional and organic intellectuals to create the counterhegemony and then gain support of the masses.

Although Gramsci did not directly address race, I view his concept of "commonsense" ideas as a tool to identify ways in which domination is racially manipulated in society today. I will use television as a point of analysis because it reaches the widest cross-section of society. In the U.S., our children watch an average of three and a half hours of television per day, starting as young as eighteen months of age. This translates into twenty-four hours of TV viewing a week. If we calculate our children's viewing patterns through secondary education, we find that they will have, on average, spent 13,000 hours in the class-room and 18,000 hours in front of a TV (Chen, 1995). During this viewing time the children are exposed to the following racial images on average: 75% White; 17% African American; 3% Asian Pacific; 2% Latino/Hispanic; 2% Other; 2% not known; 2% Native American (Children Now, 2001, 2003). Comedy programs have the least diverse cast; yet these are the primary viewing choices of young children. In addition, the majority of diverse casting is in drama programming aired after 10 p.m. Young children have this narrow lens to adopt role models on American television.

U.S. Demographic-Diversity of Children reports that in the U.S. 65% of children identify as White; 16% Latino/Hispanic; 14% African American; 4% Asian Pacific; and 1% as Native American. According to the Children Now 1996 report "Through the Eyes of a Child," the number of children in the news were 64% White; 22% African American; 12% Latino/Hispanic; and 2% Asian American. Although on the surface these numbers do not seem grossly dissimilar, analysis of the context of these news reports was disturbing. "Through the Eyes of a Child" (Children Now, 1996) reported:

African American and Latino children were more likely than other children to be placed in the context of violence;

62% of the stories aired involved African American and Latino youth focused on crimes involving weapons, assault, and the taking of hostages, twice the proportion of stories about White youth in similar contexts;

African American and Latino children were most likely to be the subject of murder stories;

1. White children were the focus of stories about missing children;
2. White females were most likely to be depicted as victims;
3. African American males were more likely to be portrayed as
4. perpetrators of crime and violence than any other group.

U.S. media studies tell us that Whites are overrepresented in positive messaging while People of Color are overrepresented in negative messaging in both entertainment and news television (Children Now, 2000, 2003), creating a commonsense idea that Whites are better than People of Color and informing the identities of our children.

Print media have similar trends. During news coverage of Hurricane Katrina, two photos on August 30, 2005 portrayed individuals wading through water and holding grocery items in their hands. The first photo read, "Two residents wade through chest-deep water after finding bread and soda from a local grocery store after Hurricane Katrina came through the area in New Orleans, Louisiana."

Photo 1: Katrina Victims. AFP/Getty Images/Chris Grythen

The second photo read, "A young man walks through chest-deep flood water after looting a grocery store in New Orleans."

Photo 2: Katrina Victims. August 30, 2005/Associated Press

Photo 1 is of two White individuals and the term "finding" is used to describe their actions. Photo 2 is of an individual of color and the term "looting" is used to describe his actions. These terms project Whites as hardworking, who earn/find what they need to survive, with honorable and intelligent attributes, while the person of color is opportunistic and unethical.

On the basis of the commonsense notion of racial inferiority, media distortions are supporting beliefs around race and identity that privilege Whites over all other peoples. Therefore, current hegemonic ideas use race to influence these beliefs and persuade society that People of Color are less educated, make less money, have a higher rate of involvement in crime and lower ethical standards. This creates an ideology that promotes the status quo that Whites are superior to People of Color. This in turn encourages People of Color, who do not wish to be associated with these negative images, to support White power and privilege.

Racial Formation

The historical evolution of hegemony and projects "in which bodies and social structures are represented and organized" are central to Omi and Winant's (1994) racial formation theory (RFT) (pp. 66-67). Racial formation is "the sociohistorical process, by which racial categories are created, inhabited, transformed, and destroyed" (p. 55). It was first presented in response to reductionist theories that treated race as an epiphenomenon of class, ethnicity, or nation. In this theory race "is a matter of both social structure and cultural representation" (p. 56). One cannot exist without the other. Structure and representation are linked through racial projects that are "simultaneously an interpretation, representation, or explanation of racial dynamics, and an effort to reorganize and redistribute resources along particular racial line" (p. 56). How these racial projects are mediated in society present outcomes that are the processes of racial formation.

Because this process is situated in history, it has changed over time and will continue to do so in the future. Omi and Winant trace the evolution of modern racial awareness from its emergence and religious justification during the rise of European power and colonization of the Americas. The shift from religious justification to biological justification and essentialism occurred in the eighteenth and nineteenth centuries while anticolonialism and civil rights movements of the twentieth century marked the recognition that race was socially constructed and politically motivated.

Prior to the Civil War, only Whites were allowed to engage in U.S. politics. Omi and Winant define this as a time of racial dictatorship (p. 65). They identify three key consequences of the period: (1) American identity as White; (2) organization of the colorline; (3) consolidation of oppositional racial consciousness and organization (p. 66). After the Civil War a transition to democracy began that is still in progress today. The ruling class historically and currently is White and dominates all others. Omi and Winant introduce hegemony to explain how this is possible. They "locate the origins of hegemony right within the heart of the racial dictatorship" (p. 67), using the example of slaves taking the religious and philosophical tools of the oppressor to gain emancipation. So dictatorship and domination led to democracy and hegemony. It is at this point that "hegemonic forms of racial rule—those based on consent—eventually supplant those based on coercion" (p. 67). Specific political projects concerning class, gender, and sex are not omitted in RFT but referred to as "regions" of hegemony just as race is a region, each intersecting and mediating the others.

Racism

Omi and Winant use RFT to present a reformulated concept of racism. First, race and racism are differentiated. They stress that the two terms should not be interchanged and that not all racial projects are racist. They present race as having "no fixed meaning, but is constructed and transformed sociohistorically through competing political projects, through the necessary and ineluctable link between the structural and cultural dimensions of race in the U.S." (p. 71). For a racial project to be racist, it must "create or reproduce structures of domination based on essentialist categories of race" (p. 71). Omi and Winant are careful to differentiate between essentialism and strategic essentialism. Essentialism works toward domination while strategic essentialism works toward emancipation. Second, they address the debate surrounding whether racism is structural or ideological. They argue that "ideological beliefs have structural consequences and that social structures give rise to beliefs, therefore racial ideology and social structure mutually shape the nature of racism in a complex, dialectical, and overdetermined manner" (pp. 74-75).

Omi and Winant do not believe that racism is only a White problem. They discuss how Jewish and Arab peoples can be victims of racism by both Whites and People of Color and argue that racism and racial political projects are not all equal. For instance, White supremacists hold more power to coerce other groups because they use dominant hegemonic discourse to rearticulate their ideologies, creating standards and norms in society. In fact, they hold that today racial hegemony is not only messy but complex and rooted in the historical inequities—structural and ideological—that have emerged since World War II (pp. 75-76). It is made up of "multipolarities of racial identities" (p. 158) that cross and weave with gender and sex. They conclude that although racism and White supremacy exist today, "the achievement of victim status (by People of Color), beginning in earnest around the turn of the century, was a challenge to White supremacy in some ways as serious as the civil rights and egalitarian challenges of the post–World War II period" (p. 158) and that these events demand that today we notice race, see race, and challenge racism rather than live in a color-blind society.

White Supremacy

Scholars of critical race and pedagogy have recently called for a critical analysis of White privilege (Allen, 2005; Bonilla-Silva, 2005; Leonardo, 2005). Omi and Winant present White supremacy as a specific racial project whereas scholars of critical race and pedagogy present it as the underlying structure that allows racial hierarchies and racism to exist and proliferate both globally and nationally from which White privilege is an outcome. Zeus Leonardo argues in Critical Pedagogy and Race (2005) that

> A critical look at white privilege, or the analysis of white racial hegemony, must be complemented by an equally rigorous examination of white supremacy, or the analysis of white racial domination. This is a necessary departure because although the two processes are related the conditions of white supremacy make white privilege possible. In order for white racial hegemony to saturate everyday life, it has to be secured by a process of domination, or those acts, decisions, and policies that white subjects perpetrate on people of color. (p. 37)

Terms such as "White privilege" and "White power" are used primarily by Whites discussing Whiteness studies. These are terms that White liberals can feel good about using; they assist in an idealist belief that equity is just around the corner. White conservatives can accept these terms as outcomes of capitalism and living in a meritocracy, I present these as safe White words in the discussion of race and racism. The terms can be useful and productive as a place to begin discussions with Whites on their racial reality, but when they are the sole focus of antiracist work they simply mask the root assumptions of White supremacy from which they evolved, giving the illusion that racial equity is currently in action. It is, therefore, understandable why so few alliances have been forged between critical race scholars of color and critical White scholars. Ricky Lee Allen addresses this phenomenon in *Whiteness and Critical Pedagogy* (2005). In his analysis of why People of Color on the U.S. educational left have difficulty accepting critical pedagogy, he argues that "our (Whites) diminution of race has alienated those who do not have the privilege to ignore White supremacy—no matter what economic form it takes" (p. 54).

This movement marks a departure from the ideological focus of Omi and Winant's RFT and recognition of the need to move toward a more general concept of racialized social systems (Bonilla-Silva, 2005) as a way to understand racial phenomena. Bonilla-Silva argues that racialized social systems refer to "societies in which economic, political, social, and ideological levels are partially structured by the placement of actors in racial categories or races" (p. 11). He uses the term White supremacy as a "shorthand" for the concept of racialized social systems "since they emerged as part of the momentous expansion of the world-system in the fifteenth and sixteenth centuries which included the development of global white supremacy" (Balibar & Wallerstein, 1991; Mills, 1997).

Bonilla-Silva (2005, pp. 17-18) presents "New Racism" as a series of elements that have developed since the 1960s and constitutes our new racial structure. They are

- The increasingly covert nature of racial discourse and racial practices;
- The avoidance of racial terminology and the ever-growing claim by Whites that they experience reverse racism;
- The elaboration of a racial agenda over political matters that eschews direct racial references;
- The invisibility of most mechanisms to reproduce racial inequality;
- The rearticulation of some racial practices characteristic of the Jim Crow period of race relations.

White supremacy now is a structural term used to understand racial phenomenon, and the elements, tenants, and root assumptions of New Racism can be used as tools of analysis when discussing racial ideology, discourse, and outcomes. This is not to say that racial projects as presented by Omi and Winant (1997) are not useful tools of analysis. They simply are one way of looking at larger racial phenomena within a White supremacist structural theory where White racial hegemony and White racial domination are a racial reality.

White Racial Projects and U.S. Policy

Omi and Winant's racial projects are a useful tool in examining how White privilege and the associated power outcomes of White supremacy are shaped. This is presented in detail by Winant in *Behind Blue Eyes: Whiteness and Contemporary U.S. Racial Politics* (2004). Using racial projects as a lens, he "examines racial politics and culture as they shape the status of whites" (p. 3) in the post–civil rights era. He calls it the "new politicization of whiteness" and analyzes Whiteness through current political projects. As I stated earlier, racial projects are a critical component to RFT (Omi & Winant, 1994) and can be classified by historical and/or current political ideology. Winant focuses on five racial projects he argues are key to understanding how meaning is made of Whiteness and White identities. They are the far right, new right, neoconservative, neoliberal, and new abolitionist, each of which I will review and encapsulate below.

The Far Right

To Winant this is the "cornerstone of white identity," grounded in the belief in "unalterable differences between Whites and People of Color" (p. 6). It is characterized by traditional beliefs of biological superiority and modernizing tendencies of fascism and neofascism. Fascists openly support Nazi and separatist racial ideologies. Neofascists advocate White supremacy and White nationalism based on racial grounds. Therefore, if there is a group to advance people of color, there should be a group to advance Whites. They view themselves as victims of an inequitable racial system that privileges People of Color through government-supported financial incentives.

The New Right

Winant (2004) grounds the new right in the "resistance" to the Black movement of the 1950s and 1960s. The new right, as with the far right, also holds that Whites are disenfranchised, but they differ on three key issues (p. 7):

1. It presents racism and White supremacy covertly through the use of coded words rather than overtly;
2. It accepts and embraces mainstream political activity;
3. It can accept some non-White social and political participation and membership if it is "color-blind" and adheres to the authoritarian nationalist formula.

The Wallace campaign of 1968 successfully resulted in the formation of a right-wing populous aware of the existing racial hierarchy and the power associated with that hierarchy for Whites. The new right knows that to keep the status quo, they must present White ideology as normal and thus coerce People of Color to accept their values, morals, and beliefs as truth.

The Neoconservative

Neoconservatives use universalism and individualism, which deny racial difference, to preserve their power and privilege and support the status quo. Universalism allows for the language and terms of equity and democracy to be applied in issues of race but does not account for undeniable inequitable outcomes in society. This is accomplished by focusing on individual rights over collective rights. In matters of race, neoconservatives adhere to an antistatist and laissez-faire ideology, opting to recognize and accept ethnicity paradigms. Winant (2004) presents Williams' (1982) analysis that neoconservatives "argue that the state cannot ameliorate poverty through social policy, but in fact exacerbates it" (p. 8), effectively causing society to question if racial inequities can be tracked in society. This conflicts with census and public employee demographic data collection, which races each of us on a daily basis.

The Neoliberal

Neoliberals also deny racial differences but rather than preserve their position they present a need to limit it. The neoliberal response to race- and class-based forms of subordination is to "systematically narrow the differences that divide working- and middle-class people as a strategy for improving the 'life chances' of minorities who are disproportionately poor" (p. 9). So neoliberals focus on social rather than cultural structures in society. This allows for class-based arguments concerning equity to proliferate. Central to the success of neoliberalism is its attention to the need for a transracial political agenda. Yet its unwillingness to address the structural components of White supremacy gives little substance to that agenda and, in fact, can be viewed as a new form of coercion to promote White racial hegemony.

The New Abolitionist

This project stresses "the invention of whiteness as a pivotal development in the rise of U.S. capitalism" (Omi & Winant, 1994 p. 10) and accepts the reality of White supremacy in society. In addition, it recognizes the construction of Whiteness as central to the rise and continuation of capitalistic rule. Abolitionists work to reject White privilege and identity through critical analysis of what Whiteness means and becoming "race traitors" or those that "refuse to collude with white supremacy" (p. 11). Although new abolitionists "adhere to a social construction model of race, they employ it chiefly to argue against biologistic conceptions of race, which is fine; but they fail to consider the complexities and roots of social construction, or as I term it, racial formation" (p. 11). Winant argues that due to the complexity of Whiteness it would be more productive to rearticulate it rather than reject it.

Each of these racial projects gives us insights into how Whites identify with political agendas to make meaning of their existence. Inherent in each is the need for Whites to address the structural components of racial formation in the U.S. (rooted in White supremacy) if we want a racially equitable society. To begin such a process is to look at social structures, such as public education, and analyze them not only from local perspectives but also state, national, and when possible, international ones. Where we fit in a broader view of society will assist us in identifying the forces that keep us from transforming systems that reproduce cycles of inequity.

Early Childhood Academic Success and Racial Ideology

Up to this point we have looked at the major theories, structures, and projects surrounding ideology and race. But what do they look like? And what are the resultant impacts on our daily lives? I will discuss this through a review of qualitative and quantitative data that exposes how our public educational system supports White power and privilege that manifests itself in White supremacy. This is accomplished through the reproduction of White racial ideologies in our schools and exemplified by the widely publicized achievement gap.

Nationally

In 2002, Frankenberg and Lee published their findings on racial segregation in U.S. metropolitan countywide districts in *Race in American Public Schools: Rapidly Resegregating School Districts*. They analyzed enrollment data collected by the U.S. Department of Education in the NCES Common Core of Data from the school year 2000 to 2001, examining the 239 school districts with total enrollment greater than 25,000 and found that "[S]ince 1986, in almost every district examined, black and Latino students have become more racially segregated from whites in their schools" (p. 4). Frankenberg and Lee drew upon the work of Orfield[2] (1995) when they concluded that "minority schools are highly correlated with high-poverty schools and these schools are also associated with low parental involvement, lack of resources, less experienced and credentialed teachers, and higher teacher turnover—all of which combine to exacerbate educational inequality for minority students" (p. 6).

Linda Darling-Hammond synthesizes current statistics and law suits serving primarily urban inner city schools in *From Separate but Equal to No Child Left Behind: The Collision of New Standards and Old Inequalities* (2004) when she states, "[S]chools serving large numbers of low income and students of color have larger class sizes, fewer teachers, and counselors, fewer and lower quality academic courses, extracurricular activities, books, materials, supplies, and computers, libraries, and special services" (pp. 6-7). Her findings are supported by the Condition of Education NCES report, which documented that nationally

> Black and Hispanic students are more likely to be concentrated in high-poverty schools. Six percent of Black and Hispanic fourth graders were in the lowest-poverty schools (with 10% or less of students eligible) in 2003 versus 29% of White fourth graders. In contrast, 47% of Black and 51% of Hispanic fourth graders were in the highest-poverty schools (with more than 75% eligible) versus 5% of White fourth graders. (p. 4)

The relationships between these factors highlight the widely publicized achievement gap between Whites and People of Color. The NAEP reported in 2004 that in both the fourth- and eighth-grade reading assessments Whites and Asian/Pacific Islander students averaged higher scores than their American Indian, Hispanic, and Black peers.[3] The same results were reported in science, math, geography, history, and writing. These trends have shown little change historically. In addition, national racial percentages (see Figure 1) report that 90% of elementary school teachers are White, while only 60% of the students they teach are White. The White teacher to White student ratio nationally is 1.5:1 while the teacher of Color to student of Color ratio is a disturbingly low .25:1.

Figure 1: 2002–2003 NCES Teachers/Students by Race/Ethnicity

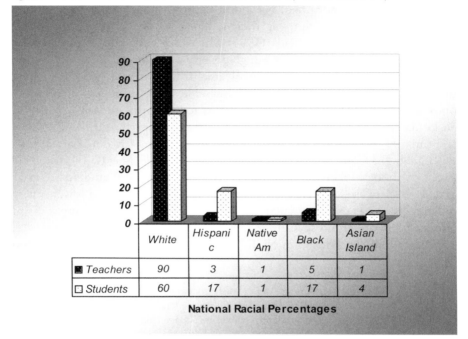

	White	Hispanic	Native Am	Black	Asian Island
■ Teachers	90	3	1	5	1
□ Students	60	17	1	17	4

National Racial Percentages

In the State of New Mexico

These statistics are consistent with state and local information. For example, in the state of New Mexico, the National Assessment of Educational Progress reported that in fourth grade, White students had an average scale score in math, reading, science, and writing that was higher than those of Hispanic, Black, and American Indian students, and the percentage of White students performing at or above the proficient level was greater than those of Hispanic, Black, and American Indian students. The gap grew in math and writing in eighth grade by 30%.[4]

On the state level White teachers make up 66.1% of the teacher workforce, yet only 32.8% of their students are White (see Figure 2). Although the percentage of Hispanic teachers greatly increases in New Mexico in comparison to national statistics, it still does not negate the fact that the White teacher to White student ratio of 2:1 still privileges White students over all other groups. In New Mexico the White teacher to White student ratio is 2.9 times higher than the Hispanic teacher to Hispanic student ratio of .7:1, 5 times higher than the Asian teacher to Asian student of .4:1, and 6.7 times higher than the Native American teacher to Native American student ratio of .3:1. Most disturbing is that it is 29 times higher than the Black teacher to Black student ratio of .07:1.

Figure 2: 2003–2004 New Mexico DCIS PK –4 Public School Teachers/Students by Race/Ethnicity

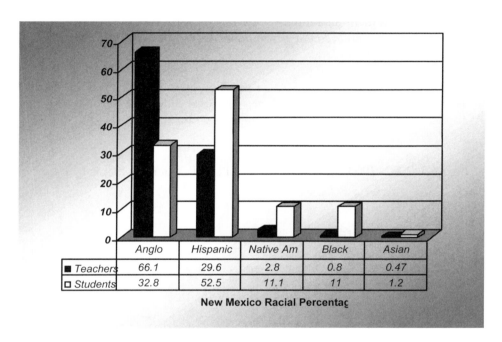

	Anglo	Hispanic	Native Am	Black	Asian
■ Teachers	66.1	29.6	2.8	0.8	0.47
□ Students	32.8	52.5	11.1	11	1.2

New Mexico Racial Percentaç

Albuquerque Public Schools System

The 2003 "Achievement Gap Report"[5] prepared by the Albuquerque Partnership reports the following statistics for the 2001-2002 Albuquerque Public Schools year:

Hispanic, African American, and Native American students' scores are significantly lower than Anglo students' scores in all grades and all content area, with Native Americans scoring the lowest.

1. Comparing the gap for Hispanics and Anglos in the third grade and the ninth grade in reading shows an achievement gap of 20.7 percentile points in the third grade and 20.9 in the ninth grade.

2. Comparing the gap in the third and ninth grade in mathematics for An-
    glos and Hispanics shows a gap of 16.1 percentile points in the third grade
    and 21.5 in the ninth grade.
3. The Native American/Anglo gap in the third and ninth grade in reading
    is 30.2 and 28 percentile points.
4. In mathematics, the third and ninth grade gap for Native Ameri-
    can/Anglo is 24 and 27.1 percentile points.
5. The achievement data indicate that for the 2001-2002 school year, there is
    a significant achievement gap among Anglo students and Hispanic and
    other minority students.

White teachers comprise 70% of the Albuquerque Public Schools teachers
(see Figure 3), while White students comprise only 37.9 % of the student
population for a ratio of 1.9:1. Teachers of Color to students of Color ratios
are closely related to the state results.

Figure 3: 2002–2003 Albuquerque RDA PK-4 Teachers/Students by Race

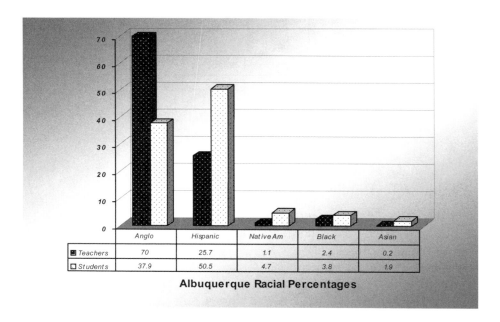

	Anglo	Hispanic	Native Am	Black	Asian
Teachers	70	25.7	1.1	2.4	0.2
Students	37.9	50.5	4.7	3.8	1.9

Albuquerque Racial Percentages

National, state, and local data on standardized measures of success in U.S.
public schools clearly place White students in overprivileged educational settings and non-White students in disprivileged educational settings both cur-

rently and historically situated. The "Albuquerque Partnership Education Achievement Gap 2004" reported that "based on the National Assessment for Educational Progress, the Education Trust publication, Education Watch, found that New Mexico students in all ethnic groups have shown little test-score progress since the 1990s" (p. 2). And as with each of the databases I examined, the results in New Mexico differ little from national trends. To support this conclusion, I draw on the work of sociologist Judith Blau—*Race in the Schools: Perpetuating White Dominance* (2003). She concludes, after analyzing ten years of two longitudinal education data sets—developed by the Department of Education's National Center for Educational Statistics and designed to measure individual variation in educational outcomes—that "the best single indicator of children's vulnerability (in school) is the color of their skin" (p. 203). This places race in society as a decisive indicator as to whom we privilege in education.

Internationally, similar results have been documented and formally linked to race. One example is the study *Education Inequality: Mapping Race, Class and Gender: A Synthesis of Research Evidence* (Gillborn & Mirza, 2000) commissioned by the Office for Standards in Education (OFSTED) in the United Kingdom. It reported a "growing gap between white pupils and their peers of Black and Pakistani ethnic origins" between 1988 and 1997 (p. 14) and that "in one large urban authority African-Caribbean pupils enter compulsory schooling as the highest achieving group but leave as the group least likely to attain five high grade GCSEs" (p. 15). This report indicates the global nature of White supremacy in education.

Gross racial inequalities are well documented in our teaching workforce, applied pedagogies, and disbursement of resources. The question now is, how do we transform public education to a system that truly strives for racial equality? In other words, how do we support RET? First, we must begin with our ideology and accept the reality of race in society, grounding ourselves in racial realism as presented by Bell. Second, we must address the structures that perpetuate White supremacy, namely White racial hegemony and RFT, to look for insights into how we can shift power positions and build alliances. Third, we must locate how we currently use racial political projects in teacher education and assess whether or not they support equity or domination. Fourth, we need to identify what root assumptions would guide a truly anti-White supremacist professional develoment project and what such a project would look like in pracitical terms. It is critical to structual change that theory is direcly linked to practical applications if we wish to move transformative pedagogoies and agendas forward. I posit that through anti-White supremacist professional develoment, we can begin the process of changing the currently accepted norm in society of racially inequitable teaching to one of racially equitable teaching.

CHAPTER 3

White Racial Ideology, Professional Development, and Racial Projects

I will present in this chapter the interconnection between White racial ideologies, professional development, and the racial projects that perpetuate racially inequitable teaching in public education. Professional development supports specific pedagogies, grounded in White hegemonic ideologies, and therefore becomes a central factor in addressing how we can support RET. We must look at the underlying structures that support racialized professional development in our public education system to understand how to effect systemic change that will promote racial equity in classrooms. I will use Winant's (2003) political racial projects as a tool of analysis to explore how teacher professional development uses current rhetoric to directly support White racial hegemony.

Professional Development as Racial Projects

Governments and school districts invest large amounts of time and money on professional development to ensure that teachers are prepared to teach our children. In public education this is largely supported through Titles I, II, and III NCLB funds. NCLB is a U.S. federal law reauthorizing the Elementary and Secondary Education Act of 1965 (ESEA). Its focus is to increase student academic performance through state, local, and school accountability, teacher quality, and parental school choice. In addition, it concentrates on basic reading and literacy skills as seen in its Reading First and Early Reading First initiatives.

National mandates under NCLB are translated into state and local mandates, which inform and drive the allocation and spending of professional development funds in public schools, highlighting the highly political nature of professional development. Professional development is one of the three indicators under Title II, "Part A: Teacher and Principal Training and Recruitment Fund," of NCLB's assessment tool, High Objective Uniform State Standard of Evaluation (HOUSSE) that determines whether a teacher is

highly qualified[6] or not. Although NCLB professional development funding is grants-based and as such a voluntary program, the reality is that only
those districts with high financial security could opt out of applying for the
allocations and following the accompanying regulations. This means that Title
I schools, those with the highest needs, could never have the financial autonomy to turn down such funding. And, because teachers in Title I schools must
be highly qualified, they are given no choice but to support NCLB-approved
initiatives to keep their Title I funding.

Therefore, Title I teachers have finite and narrowly focused opportunities
for professional growth that are dictated by their local and state departments
of education to meet NCLB mandates focusing on outcomes-based competencies. In addition, we know that Title I schools have the highest concentration
of students of Color. Also, schools that have students who speak languages
other than English are dependent upon Title III grant allocations for teacher
professional development. Title III funds are distributed from the Office of
English Language Acquisition (OELA) and dependent upon English profi-
ciency assessments, not dual or multilanguage assessments. As such, professional development is a form of racialized coercion in education perpetuated
by the government through NCLB. So we must ask, how can the government
accomplish this systemic infusion of White hegemony through professional
development? One way is to focus on the current political agendas that support this racialized coercion. I will present a racial analysis of professional development theories grounded in separatism, behaviorism, constructivism,
multiculturalism, and antiracism.

Two dominant views of professional development drive design and implementation in schools today. They are behaviorist and constructivist theories. Behaviorist is "any action taken by practicing teachers to develop their
knowledge, skills, or habits of mind toward the purpose of improving instruction," and the constructivist is "[A] purposeful educational program designed
to engage teachers in developing their knowledge, skills, or habits of mind"
(Richardson & Anders, 2005, p. 206), the key difference being the use of the
term purposeful.

To constructivists, simply participating in actions to build absolute knowledge through discrete skills acquisition does not mean one has improved capacity to teach. It is critical to the constructivist that an individual has
identified a purpose, dependent upon a process that initiates new learning for
each action undertaken in classroom teaching, weighing if the new instructional process has long-term benefits to the students. It is the individual's
processing of stimuli from the environment and the resulting cognitive structures that produce adaptive behavior, rather than the stimuli themselves

(Dewey, 1933, 1998; Harnard, 1982). In contrast, the behaviorist relies on immediate, absolute outcomes as a sign of improved instruction regardless of its long-term effects on students.

One example of the competing theories is the phonics/whole-language debate. A constructivist would argue to infuse phonics within a whole language program that emphasizes critical thinking and discussion to ensure literacy skills that assist in promoting social and academic mobility. A behaviorist would argue that applying phonics early, presenting the information in discrete skill sets, and allowing large blocks of time for the teaching of knowledge subsets will ensure basic literacy skills for all learners, a tenet of NCLB's Reading First initiative. The behaviorist views the growing gap between basic and advanced literacy skills as a normal and natural part of education, where the constructivist views it as an area that can and must be improved through purposeful teaching and professional development that stresses process and construction of new knowledge relevant to the learner. These definitions encompass traditional professional development that focuses on curriculum-specific workshops and in-service training grounded in behavior theory as well as nontraditional professional development that includes inquiry, study groups, and literature circles grounded in constructivist theory.

A commitment to issues of social justice and equity is missing from these dominant views. Multiculturalism and antiracism fill this gap: where multiculturalism encompasses all isms, antiracism acknowledges their importance, but privileges race as the ultimate structure in need of change to achieve social justice and equity. This distinction has made multicultural education more acceptable to the general public, which has been indoctrinated into White hegemony, allowing for a myriad of justifications for racial inequality. Applying antiracist professional development would mean Whites would have to accept that they have power and privilege due to structural racial inequalities in our country, which clashes with dominant views of capitalism and meritocracy. For this reason, antiracist professional development has predominately been voluntary and privately funded. Although public entitlement and grants-based education funds are used for multicultural professional development, it has historically been precipitated by a lawsuit based on racial and/or linguistic segregation, as I will discuss in detail later. Finally, White national separatism, as a form of professional development, allows the far right to perpetuate White supremacy. And as antiracism is funded predominately through private and voluntary participation, each of these professional development paradigms is supported by specific political agendas, which is outlined and discussed below (see Table2). It is important to note that these professional development projects should be viewed as phases that we move between at various points in our lives and can overlap at any time.

Political Racial Project (Winant, 2003)	Professional Development Racial Project (Earick, 2006)	Key Terms	Primary PD Funding Sources
The Far Right	Separatism	White Nationalism White Supremacy Genetic Inferiority	Private
The New Right	Behavioralism	Absolute Knowledge Outcomes-Based National Standards NCLB	Title I, II, III Vouchers Charter Schools
The Neoconservative	Constructivism	Universalism Individualism Critical Thinking Creativity Authentic Assessment NCLB	Title I, II Lawsuits Magnet and Charter Schools
The Neoliberal	Multiculturalism	Transracial Agenda Limiting Power Improved Life Chances Class-based	Title I, II, III Lawsuits Magnet and Charter Schools
The New Abolitionist	Antiracism	White Supremacy Social Justice Rejection of Whiteness	Private

Table 2: Racialized Nature of Professional Development

The Far Right and Separatist Professional Development

The far right believes in biological characteristics that make White Europeans supreme, thus the term White supremacists. They openly discuss their right to advocate for White racial nationalism, which acknowledges their superior intelligence and ownership of the U.S. state over People of Color. They justify this as a response to People of Color advocacy groups. They do not distinguish between advocacy as a form of self-promotion and advocacy as a form of social justice. To the far right, the promotion of Whites as superior is social justice. The sophistication of White supremacy today is made clear by Jared Taylor, founder and chief editor of *American Renaissance*, when he states during his interview in *Contemporary Voiced of White Nationalism in America* that the purpose of his publication is to "discuss issues that are of interests to whites" and "that it is legitimate for an organization or publication to in fact speak for them" (Swain, 2003, p.5). Taylor, a Yale graduate with international degrees, uses pseudoscience to make racism appear natural and calls his colleagues "race realists" (Fogg, 2006). These race realists were presenters at *American Renaissance*'s Seventh Biennial International Conference in Virginia in February of 2006 and included Nick Griffin. Griffin is chairman of the British National Party (BNP). During 2006 he was found innocent on two charges of inciting racial hatred in the BBC documentary, The Secret Agent (2004), where he stated that the Islam faith was "wicked" and "hateful"; this verdict has resulted in some government officials calling for a review of existing laws. Taylor further explains that,

> At the heart of our race problems is the assumption that in the United States today that when nonwhite groups—specifically blacks but also including Hispanics—when nonwhite groups are less successful in America, their differences in achievement when compared to whites must be attributed to white racism and white wickedness. I think that, by and large, this is a mistake. I think that the different racial groups are different biologically, and they differ on average in their intelligence, and that's, of course, why we never have this problem with Asians.

> (Swain, 2003, p.91)

He goes on to discuss how "nonwhites" are genetically inferior and that this fact has been proved repeatedly by the well-documented IQ testing initiated after World War II. In addition, he states that it is normal and acceptable for the Europeans who founded the U.S. to protect and propagate their lineage as well as publicly opposing interracial marriages personally and as the Chairman of the NBP.

Advocacy for White Nationalism in education is openly discussed in forums such as the monthly publication *American Renaissance*, through articles reposted from outside sources as well as from member writers. Each article has a comment board and e-mail links to respondents. An article from Rueters (Elsner, 2006) entitled Home-Schooling Growing in the United States received the following postings:

This is a move in the right direction, towards total white separation from the crumbling American Empire. Secession and self-determination are the future for white Americans.

(William at 9:11 p.m., March 3, 2006)

This is the monkey wrench in the works. Home schooling is something the powers that be never thought about. This is the way that whites can have all white schools and not have to be stuck around minorities.

(superwhite at 12:38 a.m., March, 4, 2006)

How long will it be before home schooling is outlawed for beingracist, or for denying the children the oppurtunity to experi[a]nce dive[r]sity? I cannot imagine going to a school inside a large city these days with the rampant hatred and violence directed toward white students by the black majority. In my city {Columbus Ohio, Columbus local School District} if a student wants to home school, the school system will supply the computer used to link to the online school, and send you a check for the ISP connection every month. If living inside Columbus, this is the only way to go, to insure a childs safety, or even survival. Get your kids out of any city school {Especially Columbus Schools!!!} that has more th[a]n a 33% black student population. The childs life may depend on it.

(LaShawn and Moeisha at 2:39 a.m., March 4, 2006)

These quotes are a small sampling of the responses posted and represent the White supremacist ideologies of the far right readership that is often associated with the term "White Pride" as seen on the symbol used on Stormfront, one of the first hate sites on the Internet (see Figure 4). The symbol was first used and introduced as a hate symbol by the National Front in England and was adopted by David Duke's mentee Don Black, to become Stormfront's calling card.

Figure 4: Stormfront

Most disturbing, however, is Stormfront's Education and Homeschooling Forum. It provides information, materials, and networking capabilities to like-minded White Americans to promote and preserve White supremacy. Like *American Renaissance*, it provides a venue for subscribers and readers to react to, and post, perspectives on articles printed to promote social justice to build solidarity and increase its membership. This marks a clear separatist movement in education by the far right. And through organizations such as American Renaissance and Stormfront, materials and conferences are provided to assist in the homeschool either full time or part time by parents. This constitutes a form of professional development grounded in White separatism. This epistemology encourages and supports White families as they apply racist pedagogies that propagate White supremacy. And like public education, these homeschooled children are instructed primarily by White women.

Female White supremacist Web sites present several interpretations of a woman's role in the family. They range from Her Race, housed at Stormfront, which presents traditional and extremist female perspectives, to Woman for Aryan Unity, one of the first ultraconservative Web sites for White women. The common thread in all articles is the need to fulfill the expectation that the ultimate purpose of a woman is to promote and perpetuate their race. This can take on many forms, from childbirth to politics, to activism, but the most important role highlighted is the education of future generations of White children.

For the far right the epistemology of White nationalism through separatism is the most efficient way to educate their children. One may think they would use vouchers or charter programming, but these government incentives can be used by all racial groups, and as such, interfere with their ability to practice White supremacy. Voucher and charter programs are also accountable under antidiscrimination laws, which make them unacceptable. This position is communicated succinctly by one reader at *American Renaissance* when he writes

> Well-to-do whites can send their kids to private schools, while others who flinch at throwing their children into the snakepit known as public education in America have only homeschooling as their last resort. Since white philanthropists seem to have plenty of money to give scholarships to black children to attend private primary and secondary schools, why can't scholarships be provided for white children as well? For the answer, read an article in Amren's archives entitled, "Competitive Altruism and White Destruction." In light of the increasingly leftist orientation of most teachers in all schools, both public and private (they all feed from the same trough), maybe those sending their children to expensive private schools are the ones fooling themselves about the quality of the education their children are receiving!

> (John, J. at 2:28 a.m., March 9, 2006)

The New Right and Behaviorist Professional Development

The new right is grounded in a belief that Whites are disenfranchised, present racism covertly through coded words, accept mainstream politics, and participate in sociopolitical events with People of Color as long as all members accept and adhere to a color-blind ideology (Omi & Winant, 1994; Winant, 2003). The new right promotes equity as a movement that must include a free market, standards, and God (Apple, 2001). To achieve this in education they promote party activism, national standards, and nonsecular views on the origins of life. This ensures that Whites are not disenfranchised through social programs that promote racial equity through lower class sizes, higher quality educators, recruitment of teachers of Color, and increased pay for urban public school teachers. What this translates into is growing racial segregation in our public schools, further privileging Whites. Current resource deficits in urban public schools necessitate the empowerment of teachers through higher pay and lower class sizes to counter the resource-rich suburbs that are predominately upper class, White, and draw the most experienced teachers through higher salaries and/or resource incentives. In addition, recruiting local teachers of Color would promote positive racial role models and racial in-group messaging that leads to positive academic identities in our urban schools. Therefore, the new right practices White supremacy through the promotion of racial fears, aligning with NCLB's commitment to national standards, and by building a network of political advocates in positions of power to support their views.

The ability of the new right to organize and achieve this is apparent in the power it currently exerts over book publishers and international health organizations in the area of sex education. In 2004, the Texas State Board of Education (SBOE) approved high school health textbooks that included no information about birth control and the prevention of sexually transmitted diseases (STDs) except through abstinence (Texas Freedom Network, 2006). This was accomplished through the election of new right activists to the SBOE and carefully orchestrated local and national debates based on portraying sex as evil and salacious (Bates, 2004). In addition, marriage was defined as a commitment between a man and woman; statistics on the size of gay and lesbian populations were omitted; and derogatory correlations between deviant behavior and nonheterosexual activities were presented.

One writer for the textbook companies who was reviewed was Dr. McIlhaney, a Texas physician and founder of the Medical Institute for Sexual Health. He promotes abstinence-only-until-marriage policies, and he asserted that condoms do not prevent the spread of STDs, including HIV. President George W. Bush appointed Dr. McIlhaney to the President's Council on HIV/AIDS. In addition, President Bush appointed Margaret Spellings to the position of Secretary of Education, another supporter of abstinence-only-until-marriage programs. Spellings has been a key advisor in developing domestic and education policy and assisted the president in increasing the funding for abstinence-only-until-marriage programs. These views have been incorporated into national and international HIV/AIDS education programs. In June of 2006, Representatives Luis Gutierrez (D-IL) and Jim Moran (D-VA) introduced the Guarantee of Medical Accuracy in Sex Education Act (GMA) to counter misleading and inaccurate medical information on the use of condoms, pregnancy, HIV/AIDS, and others. They have estimated that close to 800 million taxpayer dollars have been spent on these programs since 2001 with another $207 million slated for 2007. In September of 2006 it was referred to the House Education and Workforce subcommittee on educational reform. At the end of each two-year congressional session any bills and or resolutions that have not been passed are simply removed from the records. Whether this bill passes is undecided at the time of this writing, but it exposes another example of how the new right uses government appointments to promote religious propaganda in the name of educational equity.

Focusing educational and professional development of teachers on direct instruction with content-based outcomes and assessment is one way the new right can maintain White racial hegemony and use the current mainstream policies of NCLB as a means of justification. This form of professional development allows for a canon of knowledge sanctioned by the government to become absolute. Controlling the information in textbooks, as the new right has temporarily accomplished in health education, ensures the perpetuation of a White Christian epistemology. This control supports White supremacy by legitimizing and normalizing pro-life beliefs and portraying gay and lesbian lifestyles as deviant through the teaching of health science. By virtue of NCLB, teachers have been instructed in the name of educational equity to teach only what will increase test scores. Teachers hesitate to add or change approved official curriculum in fear of not covering mandated content and/or facing sanctions by their administration. This is especially true in urban schools where scripted curriculums such as DISTAR (Direct Instruction System for Teaching Arithmetic and Reading), Success for All, and Reading Mastery have become dominant forms of instruction. Direct instruction in a content area became the focus of professional development in the late 1980s after the National Institute of Education published *Teaching as Clinical Information Processing* (Gage, 1975) and became the basis of the design and implementation of traditional professional development projects grounded in behavioralism. Correlation studies emerged measuring behaviors and traits between teachers and student performance (Brophy & Good, 1986; Gage, 1978; Stallings, Needels, & Stayrook, 1980), which resulted in an examination of reading and mathematical subject-specific content (Good & Grouws, 1979).

The ensuing recommendations were to increase emphasis on direct instruction and time on task (Fisher et al., 1980), to increase absolute content knowledge of teachers, which would then be replicated in classrooms with students. These recommendations were applied to all content areas and promised equal and equitable learning environments through a system of content-knowledge assessment and modifications based on identified areas of deficiency.

Behaviorists (Guetherie, 1945; Ormond, 2004; Pavlov, 1927; Skinner, 1948) believe in equipotentiality, that animals and humans learn in similar ways, and that for this reason we can apply our knowledge of animal behavior to humans. Thought processes are not reliable subjects for research because they cannot be observed, whereas environmental stimuli and organism response can be, allowing documenters to be objective and scientific. This puts forth the argument that all humans are equal in their ability to access and accommodate knowledge. Sex, gender, race, and culture are not variables that affect one's ability to learn if the correct stimuli and predetermined response is presented. These beliefs held by behaviorists (i.e., that there is absolute knowledge, that it is possible to be objective, and that we have common learning modes, regardless of social or racial inequities) exemplify how what one says differs from what one does, representing a color-blind ideology. Although behaviorists ground their work in equity through objectivity, they ignore the sociocultural aspect of access and accommodation of knowledge production. Through their actions they communicate that race does not matter.

Key to this method of professional development is identifying what content is assessed that gives the testing agency power over what is considered absolute knowledge. Therefore, the production of knowledge is in the control of the educational system that selects and authorizes the testing agencies, which we know privileges White, upper middle class Eurocentric, and heterosexual males. And as the Texas health book adoptions have shown, they must also be Christians. Currently in the U.S. public schools, White racial hegemony is practiced and supported through behaviorist or outcomes-based professional development that deems you deficient if you do not accept their interpretation of knowledge.

The Baldridge Model

So what does this form of professional development look like in schools? Business models of professional development are behaviorist-based and are gaining acceptance in public schools. The Baldridge in Education initiative is a prime example of how content- or outcomes-based teaching is a driving force in our educational system. Currently this initiative is operating in multiple states to include Illinois, Indiana, Maryland, New Mexico, Ohio, and Texas public schools, predominately in schools performing at the lowest levels in each state. The "Malcolm Baldridge Criteria for Performance Excellence" was created in 1987 and named posthumously for former Secretary of Commerce Malcolm Baldridge. Originally it was designed to help American business and industry gain a competitive edge in the global market. In the 1990s the education version of the criteria was designed as a "framework for understanding and improving school performance and student learning." And in 2004 the National Institute of Standards and Technology (NIST) was authorized to expand the Malcolm Baldridge National Quality Award Program to nonprofits and government agencies when President Bush signed legislation into law lending valuable government support of this model in both public and private sectors.

It is a business model that has eleven core values embedded in seven categories. Central to this model is PDSA (Plan, Do, Study, Act). Charts are kept on each student and these charts help to assess what the students need to do to increase their test scores. On the now defunct Baldridge in education Web site, Rose Ann McKernan Executive Director of Research, Development, and Accountability (RDA) in the Albuquerque Public Schools is quoted as saying, "I cannot ever express how easy this SQS (Strengthening Quality in Schools) process/training makes RDA's job!" It is a data-driven criterion that appeals to statisticians who want to document test-score growth for their NCLB performance ratings. This of course is most important to Title I schools whose funding priorities are heavily impacted by performance ratings and who are servicing urban and rural areas with disproportionate amounts of racially isolated and low socioeconomic families.

Over one year, I observed ten classrooms in two schools that use this model in an urban public school district in New Mexico. No longer were pictures of art, students' creative work, or integrated curriculum materials on the walls. Instead student test scores in chart form and sticker charts covered the walls. Educators and their student teachers regularly addressed the charts and discussed how they needed to practice more to increase the test scores. I came to realize that practice was a codeword for dittos or the old teaching to the test. When I asked teachers and administrators at each school what they thought of the program, they gave the following responses:

> It's great, the students know what to expect and don't interrupt teaching, asking a lot of questions anymore.

> It has made my job easier, parents can't blame me when their child doesn't perform well, it's all on the charts.

> I love it! My staff knows what I expect and do it. No arguing anymore.

Note the focus on controlling dissent from children, parents, and teachers. All responsibility for performance ultimately fell on individuals rather than the structures they were functioning within. Although the majority of responses were similar to these, at least two teachers in each school confided in me that they were afraid the Baldridge model was creating a curriculum with no challenges or expectations of creative and critical thought. They explained that students became bored and the only way to keep them motivated was to take privileges away. As one teacher told me, "Critical thinking, how can you have meaningful discussions or critical thinking when there is only time to test, PDSA, retest? It's all time-sensitive!" She also explained that she would not voice this opinion in her district until she had seniority in a school.

It became obvious as I observed in classrooms and spoke to teachers that the Baldridge model was a case of surveillance and control of not only students but also teachers and parents. Under this model, teacher, student, and parental expectations are based on student performance on tests and their ability to perform the PDSA. This means that if a student does not perform on traditional paper-and-pencil tests, which only measure procedural knowledge and rote ability, they are deemed deficient. I observed a teacher grading a set of math tests that would be charted, graphed, and reported to the students, families, and ultimately the administration. Five of her twenty-four students who performed a math problem with multiple steps and calculations arrived at the correct answer and simply did not remember to put the squared sign on the numeral in the equation. Their conceptual knowledge of the process was evident, but they failed that section of the test; they did not meet their goal and were categorized as deficient in that math area.

The message in each of these schools, and I fear many others who have adopted this model, is that if you do not follow directions and procedures exactly as told by your superior (teacher, administrator, central officer), you are not intelligent or successful in academic settings. We know that our curriculum is Eurocentric, and our workforce is 90% monolingual middleclass White teachers who predominately adhere to a color-blind ideology. This means the materials and assessment methods applied in schools are supporting White advancement and assimilation to White supremacist ideology for all peoples. Under the guise of fairness and accountability, Baldridge has been applied to coerce People of Color to accept White ideologies through assimilation and indoctrination into a system of directions, procedures, and predetermined expectations that keep the status quo. If a student and his or her family do not have the information or power to counter the PDSA and testing charts, they have no choice but to adhere to this system in fear of being held back for additional remediation.

When my son did not read on the prescribed level in first through third grade I was given the option to hold him back or let him pass on. I, of course, passed him knowing that not all children learn decoding skills in literacy at the same pace, and that his oral language indicated his comprehension was high, a key indicator to later performance. I knew this because I was an early childhood teacher with a master's degree and I had knowledge about multiple learning theories, academic identities, and alternative assessments. The average parent bogged down by the necessity of bringing food to the table typically would not have access to such information to challenge a school adopting a Baldridge model.

The Office of Bilingual Education and Minority Languages Affairs

A powerful example of this assimilation process in education was the substitution of the Office of Bilingual Education and Minority Language Affair s (OBEMLA) by the Office of English Language Acquisition (OELA) in 2001 under the Bush administration. I came across this information while researching for an Early Reading First Grant. One day I was speaking to the OBEMLA and then the next day it was the OELA. When I e-mailed to ask for clarification, I received the following message, "It's been changed"; nothing else was the response. I tried to get access to the original OBEMLA Web page, and I received no response. When I called up, I met with a recording and there was no way to have access to a live person. It left a rather hollow and 'Big Brother' feeling that I find difficult to forget. Moving the focus of the Department of Education's office from bilingualism to English Language Acquisition creates a gatekeeping mechanism for school districts that want to provide programs in the home languages of students currently living in the U.S. through Title III funds. Therefore, the $620 million dollars distributed through Title III grants to states in 2006 were dependent upon assessments of English language proficiency, not bilingualism as the OBEMLA supported prior to the authorization of the OELA. Yet in 2006 and 2007 President Bush allotted federal funds for the training of teachers and students in what the OELA has deemed "critical foreign languages" that include Arabic, Chinese, Farsi, Japanese, Korean, Russian, and Urdu. Grant initiatives to support critical foreign languages fall under the National Security Language Initiative (NSLI). These programs are outlined in Table 3.

Table 3: NSLI 2006-2007 Funding Priorities   http://www.ncela.gwu.edu/spotight/NSLI/

Defense Programs	Education Programs	Intelligence Programs	State Programs
FLAGSHIP PROGRAMS Strategic partnerships between the federal government and U.S. Institutions of Higher Education to implement programs of advanced instruction in critical languages CIVIL LINGUISTICS RESEARVE CORPS Maintain a readily available corps of certified expertise in languages determined to be important to the security of the nation	Teacher-to-Teacher Initiative Language Teacher Corps Foreign Language Assistance Program Advancing America Through Foreign Language Partnerships E-Learning Language Clearing house	STARTALK The establishment of summer language study "feeder'" programs, grants and initiatives with K-16 educational institutions In 2007 summer language programs serviced 400 HS students and 400 HS/College Teachers in five states	Fulbright Student Program Intensive Summer Language Institutes Gilman Scholarships Teacher Exchanges Fulbright Foreign Language Teaching Assistant Program Youth Exchanges (HS)
FY 06 NR*	FY 06 $22 Million	FY 06 $2.3 Million	FY 06 NR
FY 07 NR	FY 07 $57 Million	FY 07 $5 Million	FY 07 $26.7 Million

Note: *NR=Not reported in the NSLI 2007 Report

A major metaphor associated with assimilation is the melting pot. All one needs to do to succeed is to melt into one being, an American, as seen in the change from bilingual education to English language acquisition after the 2001 reauthorization of NCLB, which included the following amendment:

> AMENDMENT: 2002 - Pub. L. 107-110, Sec. 1072(c)(2)(B), *substituted* "Office of English Language Acquisition, Language Enhancement, and Academics Achievement for Limited English Proficient Students" for "Office of Bilingual Education and Minority Languages Affairs" in section catchline.
>
> Subsec. (a). Pub. L. 107-110, Sec. 1072(b), *substituted* "Office of English Language Acquisition, Language Enhancement, and Academic Achievement for Limited English Proficient Students" for "Office of Bilingual Education and Minority Languages Affairs."
>
> Subsec. (b)(1). Pub. L. 107-110, Sec. 1072(d), *substituted* "Director of English Language Acquisition, Language Enhancement, and Academic Achievement for Limited English Proficient Students" for "Director of Bilingual Education and Minority Languages Affairs."

(U.S. House of Representatives (20 USC Sec. 3423d))

Yet where the OELA was "established" (20 USC Sec. 3420), there was no reference to closing the OBEMLA, only that the OELA substituted that office, Creating a new metaphor of substitution and rearticulating a color-blind and language-blind ideology. Although a great majority would like to project that we all are part of the great American melting pot, the reality is that we are hypersegregated and geographically isolated from People of Color, substituting our ideological beliefs for theirs, President Bush states that the acquisition of a second language is necessary to spread democracy rather then diversify our own country, as communicated by the Department of Education:

> We need people in America who can go and say to people, living in freedom is not the American way of life, it is a universal way of life. We're not saying your democracy has to be like yours [ours]. We're just saying give your people a chance to live in a free society; give women a chance to live freely; give young girls a chance to be educated and realize their full potential. And the best way to do that is to have those of us who understand freedom be able to communicate in the language of the people we're trying to help. In order to convince people we care about them, we've got to understand their culture and show them we care about their culture.

(Bush, G.W., NSLI, 2006)

This interest in absolute content competencies seen in the Baldridge model and substitution of the OBEMLA by the OELA for students and teachers is presented as a way to be fair regardless of one's race, gender, or socio-economic status. Students who are excelling can move on and students who are not excelling can have deficits identified and remediated. Fairness is a code word for the status quo and remediation for racism. In this way a meritocracy epistemology is applied. For the new right, this represents the halting of programs that cater to low-performing, predominantly students of Color and provides opportunity for high-performing, predominantly White students to gain more power and privilege through advanced coursework and enhanced, faith-based curriculums. The message is, if you do not like our tests, images, and language, you must be remediated until you do. This assimilist ideology is justified through NCLB mandates for local, state, and national testing. Because Title I funding is directly related to teachers gaining their highly qualified status and Title III funding is the major source of funding for English Language Learners, their program goals and assessments are also widely accepted in urban public schools. NCLB is a structural form of coercion in our educational system that allows programs such as Baldridge's and the critical languages initiative at the OELA in the name of democracy, to become accepted curriculum models that limit the knowledge produced in school to ensure White racial hegemony with the support of political activists in the new right. They accept mainstream politics and actively participate in sociopolitical events to proselytize their White supremacist Christian beliefs throughout public education.

The Neoconservative Racial Project: Constructivist Professional Development

Neoconservatives rely on the rhetoric of universalism and individualism to preserve their power and privilege and support the status quo. Therefore, the idea that we come from a common source and have the right to liberty to act in our own defense is central. Within this paradigm there are no racial differences, but ethnicity is acknowledged and accepted as real. Neoconservatives also hold that social policies aimed at lessening poverty are impossible and only serve to worsen it. Therefore, decentralizing education through merit pay, accountability, efficiency, and competitive-for-profit programming are considered needed reforms. Their attention to the concept of creative thinking differentiates them from the far right. Rather than relying on the need for absolute knowledge, a tenet of the new right, neoconservatives believe that decentralizing schools spurs creative programming that shapes motivated and creative students.

Hess (2006), Director of Education Policy Studies at the American Enterprise Institute (AEI), presents this philosophy in *Tough Love for Schools*. AEI is the leading think tank of neoconservatives currently working as a collective in the U.S. *Tough Love for Schools* professes seven principles:

1. Hold schools and educators responsible for performance without blaming educators for all of society's ills;
2. Encourage competition through charter schools, vouchers, distance education, and other measures—because accountability alone can be stifling;
3. School districts need to work in all ways, especially in human resources and use of technology. It cannot be a good school if it is not hiring good people and supporting them once they are hired;
4. Recognize excellent educators and reward them appropriately;
5. The rules and precautions that define school districts need to be unwound. Along with choice-based reform efforts like charter schooling and supplemental services, lessening of restrictions is part of what is making it easier for educators and others to launch new, creative programs and schools;
6. We must look outside the regular channels for teachers and principals to attract those with the skills we need. Now, expertise is important, and valuable, but we should not presume we know how to deliver it. Instead, we should cultivate and support it;
7. It requires that we be reasonable about expectations. We do not expect a great teacher to ensure that a fourth grader can master algebra or write like Shakespeare. Similarly, we need to be reasonable in what we ask of schools, school systems, and educators.

Hess' seven principles have been explored and applied with varied success over the past twenty years. His assertion that they are attainable through the decentralizing and reorganizing of school structures is an example of the neoconservative denial of racial conflict and differences currently prevalent in schools. And ironically, his assertion that we should decentralize, reward, and cultivate creative programming contradicts his critique of the Bill and Melinda Gates Foundation-funded schools. In *Retooling K-12 Giving* (2004), Hess argues that "the reality that today's small schools are frequently successful as boutique institutions that (a) have students and faculty who have chosen to be there and (b) receive extensive exemptions from onerous regulations and staffing rules." These realities are models for creative, dedicated teachers supporting creative student learning.

The neoconservative views are consistent with constructivist theories (Bruner, 1996; Piaget, 1952; Vygotsky, 1986) of learning and professional development, which also stress universalism, individualism, and independence as a route to success (Dewey 1933, 1998; Harnard, 1982). Inquiry-based learning

(Postman & Weingartner, 1969) is one form of constructivist education that has historically been valued in science and math education and more recently applied to multiple content areas. Three levels of inquiry are traditionally applied in classrooms. They are structured, guided, and student-directed inquiry. Each level gives more autonomy to the students. In structured inquiry, the topic, questions, procedures, and materials are dictated by the teacher, while the student is in charge of producing results, analysis, and conclusion. In guided inquiry, students assist with the design. Student-directed inquiry consists of a teacher-generated topic and question, leaving materials selection and design up to the students. These inquiry models represent the production of knowledge that is controlled by the teachers; in each, the teacher controls the topic and questions. This is critical because teachers will argue that they are doing everything possible for all students, addressing diverse needs through inquiry-based learning and promoting fairness in their classrooms. If, however, they were dedicated to authentic critical thinking, they would introduce the fourth level of inquiry, student-initiated research, rarely seen in public education. As a supervisor of student teachers, I have worked with in-service and preservice teachers in classrooms. When I pose direct questions to the equity of their inquiry-based lessons, they discuss in detail the need to have relevant curriculum materials for their students. Yet when I ask them to expand on this, they focus on geographic, gender, and linguistic relevancy. They do not consider race or socioeconomic status.

What's in the Bag?

I observed an inquiry lesson in a fourth-grade classroom that involved using the senses to guess what was in a sealed brown bag filled with food and air. The teacher spent several hours creating small group logs, information sheets, and collecting produce, so that afterward the exercise could be used in a cooking project. This teacher felt secure that he was addressing the needs of every student in his class. He made a point of telling me prior to the observation that he even got the produce names translated into Spanish to field responses in a child's first language because he was monolingual. Though on the surface all students seemed engaged and busy, during the debriefing of the results problems arose.

The teacher had purchased the produce at the local health food store, located in a predominantly White area, and brought unusual items such as purple potatoes and star fruits, both expensive and not the traditional fair found in local supermarkets. It became obvious that the White students, the minority in the class, had many experiences shopping at the health food store and knew immediately what the items were. It also became obvious that many of the students of color (who had extensive knowledge of produce, whose families shopped primarily at the local grocery store, and grew many of their own vegetables), did not immediately identify the items. The result of this was that in each group the correct answers to this inquiry-based lesson were given by White students, primarily due to the materials chosen by the teacher. In reality, many students identified the purple potato as young or a potato with color, but the teacher gave positive messaging to only the students (White) who had the most correct answer (as he termed it) by saying "it was a purple potato." Until I shared my observation notes with him, the teacher did not realize that all correct answers were contributed by White students.

Constructivism, as seen in inquiry-based programs, universally believes that knowledge is constructed by the individual through his or her interactions with their environment, stressing one's right to liberty in learning environments. The teacher acts as guide, mentor, and facilitator while the students mediate and control knowledge construction. Overdependence on a teacher is frowned upon because it could perpetuate a cycle of dependency in the production of knowledge. In fact, ,defending one's position and debates as to "best," or in our example, "most correct" answers are considered desirable traits in constructivist classrooms. Constructivist theory subscribes to the presentation of alternative viewpoints, which is often associated with equity and democracy. Yet presenting alternative viewpoints suggests that all viewpoints are equally valued and promotes a pedagogy of tolerance rather than critical analysis. The use of the term multiple perspectives is a more accurate way to assess viewpoints because it recognizes that not all viewpoints are equal or desirable.

A shift from behavior theory to constructivist theory has recently moved professional development projects focusing on direct instruction in isolation to dealing with the relationship between process and content (Richardson, 2003). This shift stresses the need for teachers to process, apply strategies in classrooms, and reflect on teaching to change belief systems and affect long-term change in teaching practices. Yet inquiry-based teachers are adopting a neoconservative belief system. Teachers believe they simply need to provide an opportunity to explore materials and children will universally learn when, in fact, we know experiences must be relevant to the student for conceptual learning to occur. This relevancy spans their race, ethnicity, gender, sex language, and abilities. As Tobin (1991) argues, learning is interpretative and dependent upon the learner negotiating meaning, comparing past experiences, and resolving discrepancies between new and past knowledge. So although constructivists, such as inquiry-based teachers, may be moving away from a behaviorist system of beliefs, that does not mean there is equitable teaching in their classrooms. It often masks inequities because equity and democratic language such as individual learning styles, alternative assessment, differentiated teaching and fairness are used in this paradigm. This allows for the preservation of White racial hegemony within a neoconservative project that is supported by a constructivist theory. This constructivist theory stresses individual knowledge construction at the expense of collective social knowledge, and ignoring the cumulative effects of historical events on raced peoples. Therefore, inquiry as a viable pedagogy for equity is only as effective as the level of power and control students are allowed to practice. And as I have presented, it is typically a teacher-initiated and teacher-controlled task that communicates a commitment to the status quo.

The Neoliberal Racial Project: Multiculturalist Professional Development

Neoliberals focus on social rather than cultural structures in society, promoting class-based arguments concerning equity and the denial of racial differences. They acknowledge the need to limit their position of power and privilege believing the way to achieve this is by improving life chances of those disproportionately poor (Winant, 2003). Central to the success of neoliberalism is its attention to the need for a transracial political agenda. Neoliberals do not address the structural inequities that have allowed them to gain their current power and privilege status, calling into question the integrity of their transracial agenda. Multicultural education supports the concept of a transracial agenda in education without focusing on White racial hegemony. This avoids discussions around White supremacy by focusing on all isms. This allows neoliberals to support multiculturalism in the name of perceived equity, believing they are working toward their goal of limiting power and improving life chances of the poor. Yet as I have presented in previous chapters, those who benefit most from a class-based argument are White. Although Whites represent the highest number of children living in poverty, they still outperform students of Color on standard measures of success. Whites are overrepresented in curriculum materials, advanced classes, and higher education. In addition, White women are offered the most opportunities through affirmative action. This is made possible through competing perspectives on what constitutes multicultural curriculum and pedagogy due to multiple isms.

Three prominent topologies of multicultural education are content-oriented, student-oriented, and socially oriented (Banks, 1994; Sleeter & Grant, 1993). In the content-oriented topology, knowledge of cultural groups informs curriculum and educational materials with a goal of increasing students' knowledge about these groups. In its simplest form, classrooms address holidays and heroes while more sophisticated models address "single-group studies" (Sleeter & Grant, 1993) commonly based on race, ethnicity, or gender. Examples of addressing holidays and heroes would be acknowledging Martin Luther King's birthday or reading a paragraph about Rosa Parks, while examples of single-group studies would be Black History Month or women's studies. Although the student-oriented topology demands stronger content knowledge, its main goal is to increase academic achievement for an identified group (Banks, 1994). Focusing on moving linguistically diverse students into our monolingual English mainstream would be an example of a student orientation. Socially oriented programs were established to increase cross-racial contacts (Banks, 1994). They focus on "human relations" (Sleeter & Grant, 1993) in the curriculum, promote positive group messaging, and apply research on diverse learning styles to increase student achievement and decrease racial tension. Critical social multiculturalism, which acknowledges the need to shift positions of power from White racial hegemony, is not currently accepted in public schools.

The predominant multicultural topologies currently in schools are content or single-group. This is a key indicator of the neoliberal focus of multiculturalism currently at work in society and prominent in our professional development. Although culturally relevant teaching –a critically needed pedagogy- is becoming a more mainstream form of social multiculturalism, its desire to include all isms limits its effectiveness in addressing the structural mechanisms needed in society to shift positions of power from Whites to People of Color in educational settings. In her study of effective teachers of African American students, Ladson-Billings (1994) identifies six tenets of culturally relevant teaching:

1. Students, whose educational, economic, social, political, and cultural futures are most tenuous, are helped to become intellectual leaders in classrooms; (p. 117)
2. Students are apprenticed in a learning community rather than taught in an isolated and unrelated way; (p.117)
3. Students' real-life experiences are legitimized as they become part of the "official" curriculum; (p. 117)
4. Teachers and students participate in a broad conception of literacy that incorporates both literature and oratory; (p. 117)
5. Teachers and students engage in a collective struggle against the status quo; (p. 118)

6. Teachers do not accept the prevailing belief that their students will not do
well. They have high expectations for their students and convey their belief to the students. Teachers are cognizant of themselves as political beings. (p. 118)

For White teachers to embrace cultural relevancy and equitably apply
these tenets, they must first understand they are racial beings. Unfortunately
the language is often co-opted rather than used to enter into deep self-
reflective practices.

Co-opting Language

Neoliberals use cultural relevancy to promote themselves as progressive
and allied with multiracial groups. Observing and working with teachers in
New Mexico exemplifies how school districts co-opt and rearticulate theories,
such as cultural relevancy, to fit their political needs. One large urban school
district has adopted the *People and Places* social studies textbook. I witnessed its
use in kindergarten through fourth grade over one year. It was presented to
me as a culturally relevant text, adopted due to its unique inclusion of New
Mexican culture and history. The first lesson I observed was on New Mexico
communities. It presented New Mexico as primarily a Hispanic community,
with little attention paid to the Indigenous Peoples of the Americas or presenting how the term Hispanic[7] was being defined. I asked the teacher if she
felt this was a fair representation of New Mexico and she said, "Oh yes, this is
what our children experience on a daily basis, very relevant to their lives, I
should know" (referring to her self-identification as Hispanic and a liberal
educator).

I then read the integrated literature for each unit. The majority of the
authors were White presenting both dominant and nondominant perspectives. One unit focused on Colonizers and Native Americas. Colonizers were
presented as bringing technology to North America and Native Americans as
accepting these changes. In the group illustrations Colonizers (Whites) had
been drawn with unique physical features, while the Indigenous Peoples of the
Americas had similar features, making it difficult to distinguish individuals,
thus making them invisible as a social group, and promoting them as historical
caricatures. The teacher said it was a wonderful unit, very different from past
books that presented Native peoples as savages, "What a horrible thing!" I
asked her to look at the images and tell me what she thought they conveyed.
She looked puzzled. I pointed out that it was the technology of the White
colonizers that was privileged, even though the technology of the Indigenous

Peoples of this time was equally important. In addition, I discussed how each illustration portrayed unique physical features on the Whites, unlike the Indigenous Peoples who all had the same features. I asked her to look at the clothing and cultural artifacts in the text and identify what peoples were being presented. Her eyes grew wide and she looked up at me, "I never noticed, I never thought..." she replied. This teacher was trained in the use of the text and it was presented to her as culturally relevant, simply because it included local units, images, and activities. She was aware there were tenets of culturally relevant teaching. She told me, "I have a handout or something somewhere from an in-service on the topic" but she interpreted the tenets in such a way that she depoliticized their meaning. She told me the need to have appropriate context, to engage families, and have high standards but she had no idea as to how to critique materials for content both covert and overt outside her own race and culture. This school proudly stated they are culturally relevant, when in fact they have simply co-opted the language without first deconstructing their own ideologic beliefs or committing to long-term critical self-reflection, a key component of culturally relevant education.

Reactionary Interventions

Professional development programs in multicultural or antibiased education have often focused on bringing diverse groups of individuals together to discuss concerns and improve intergroup relations, supporting tolerance and cultural relevancy pedagogies. These programs are often precipitated by lawsuits based on student segregation by class and race. African American and Latino plaintiffs together with civil rights law activists in Connecticut have been arguing with the state for sixteen years to improve educational access and resource distribution to schools throughout the Hartford region. Known as the Sheff case, outcomes included two magnet schools per year to be established with an annual enrollment goal of 2400 students. These schools have met only the needs of 862 students to date. The original 1996 decision impacted schools across the state. My own school in CT, was mandated in 1997 to participate in a one-day "World of Difference" (ADL [Advanced Distributed Learning]) workshop, as were most public schools. Similar cases can be found around the country in urban districts.[8] The quality of the professional development was dependent on the workshop leaders, who themselves were not comfortable in this limited training module to discuss racial tension, and the lack of opportunity to work throughout the year with the ADL.

The problem is that the majority of these programs are add-ons or one-shot (one-day) programs. This is due to the fact that social multicultural education can make White teachers uncomfortable and professional development monies are traditionally targeted for content-based projects used by NCLB to measure academic progress. In the field of education, research has found that these programs rarely improve cross-cultural relations because the material is too brief and/or superficial. We know that little or no effects occur on teacher behavior and/or attitudes simply by presenting facts and information about other cultures (Cotton, 1993). In addition, we know that one-shots or limited relationships between teachers and antibiased programs typically do not reduce bias or prejudice (Byrnes & Kiger, 1986-1987; Garcia, Powell, & Sanchez, 1990; Gimmestad & DeChiaria, 1982; Hart & Lumsden, 1989; Merrick, 1988; Pate, 1981, 1988). In fact, these informational and one-shot projects have been shown to increase intolerance (Zeichner & Hoeft, 1995). Applying multicultural programs in this manner communicates the rhetoric of the neoliberal racial political project. Informational and one-shot projects focus on perceived transracial agendas and programs, since they ignore the overwhelmingly racial nature of educational outcomes.

New Abolitionists' Racial Project: Antiracist Professional Development

New abolitionists recognize that the construction of Whiteness is central to the rise and continuation of capitalistic rule and accept the reality of White supremacy in our society. Through critical analysis, new abolitionists consistently work to reject White privilege and identity. These are central tenets to antiracist professional development. And just as Winant critiqued abolitionists for not addressing the complexities of the structural component of racial formation, the same is true in education. This is by no means the fault of abolitionists; it is simply due to the fact that antiracist professional development traditionally occurs outside the school because of the sensitive nature of the work, something that must change. This means observable changes are rarely documented and therefore cannot be used to challenge White racial hegemony.

Historically, antiracist professional development in U.S. schools has focused on individual and cultural racism and fallen into the category of Race Awareness Training. It emerged in 1968 after the *Kern Commission Report* was published. The report found that "white society is deeply implicated in the ghetto. White institutions created it, white institutions maintain it, and white society condones it" (p. 1). The response in the U.S. was to focus on the psychology of the White as an individual. This discourse allowed structural issues of White supremacy to be ignored, allowing Whites to take on a missionary discourse during the civil rights movement. Stokely Carmichael, a Black power leader, spoke out against this missionary discourse and told Whites that if they wanted to help, they had to free their own people first (Hamilton & Carmichael, 1967).

Carmichael's comments were heard and new models of Race Awareness Training began to emerge. Most notable were the models of Bidol (1971) and Katz (1978). They focused on the cognitive components of racism, promoting the need to explore our attitudes and understandings of racism, and they recognized that institutional racism is a fundamental component of our daily lives. This represented a move from identifying one recipient of racism, People of Color, and acknowledging the unhealthy psychological effects of racism on the White perpetrators (Pettigrew, 1981; Terry, 1981). Each identified the need to move from race awareness to racism awareness, arguing that Whites do not see themselves as racial beings (Katz & Ivey, 1977) or inherently racist because they were born into a system of White-skin privilege (Bidol, 1971). However, with its focus on confronting racism and changing individual consciousness, racial awareness training does not typically concentrate on challenging structural racism. This is not to say racial awareness training does not contribute to its deconstruction. In fact, its focus on the need for Whites to accept and explore the social construction (Fine, Weis, Powell, & Mun Wong, 1997) and ensuing privileges (McIntosh, 1989) of their race has and continues to greatly contribute to the field of critical Whiteness studies.

As I stated earlier, focusing on individual and to a lesser degree cultural racism is consistent with the new abolitionist political racial project. Solomon and Levine-Rasky reported in "Transforming Teacher Education for an Antiracism Pedagogy" (1996) that "In survey responses they agree overwhelmingly that the goals of ARE [antiracist education] are to change individual behaviors and attitudes, and institutional policies and practices that reinforce and perpetuate racism. But, in follow-up interviews they diverge widely in their subjective interpretations of antiracism and its application within schools and classrooms" (p. 3). Furthermore, it has been well documented in the U.S., Canada, and the United Kingdom that most classroom teachers are ambivalent, give contradictory responses, and at times are antagonistic to antiracist projects and policies (Rizvi & Crowley, 1993; Sleeter, 1992b; Solomon & Levine-Rasky, 1994, 1996; Troyna, 1993).

Given that the majority of antiracist professional development is geared toward these classroom teachers, with little to no district support, it is not surprising that the application of antiracist pedagogies has been slow in educational settings. In fact, many theorists, politicians, and education practitioners have openly argued against antiracist projects in schools, viewing them as extremist, divisive, confrontational, ideological, and radical in relationship to much of the tolerance pedagogy in multiculturalism (Honeyford, 1986; Jeff-coate, 1984; Lynch, 1987; Marks, 1986; Palmer, 1986). The conflicting identi-ties of racist and antiracist have been the subject of much research in the field of psychology and a factor in why cross-cultural training is prominent in antib-iased curriculum and professional development rather than in antiracist train-ing. Individuals working toward equity would prefer not to be called racist, since the historical artifacts such as KKK hoods, cross-burning, and lynching cause uncomfortable and deep emotions in our society.

Race does matter in considering whom we privilege in education and this race-based privilege is enabled through teacher racial ideologies. These ideologies are made visible through pedagogies in which White teachers typi-cally place themselves in a color-blind ideology and discourse where Whiteness is normalized. Now we can also see how these ideologies are reproduced through political racial projects and manifested in professional development in our public schools. The new right is grounded in a belief that Whites are disenfranchised, present racism covertly through coded words, and accept mainstream politics such as NCLB, allowing them to maintain White racial hegemony. Neoconservatives rely on the rhetoric of universalism and indi-vidualism to preserve their power and privilege and support the status quo. This is consistent with constructivist theories of learning and professional de-velopment, which also stress universalism, individualism, and independence as a route to success. Neoliberals focus on social, rather than cultural, structures in society. This promotes a class-based argument concerning equity and the denial of racial differences, creating a transracial agenda based on economics. Multicultural education supports the concept of a transracial agenda in educa-tion without focusing on White racial hegemony. Rather it concentrates on culture and therefore avoids discussions around White supremacy. Con-versely, new abolitionists recognize the reality of White supremacy in our soci-ety and work to reject their power and privilege.

The lack of documentation and dedication to transformative antiracist professional development demonstrated by U.S. school districts communicates an ideology of color blindness, which we know will promote, rather than de-construct, racism. This ideology is then supported through professional devel-opment aligned with political racial projects such as NCLB. NCLB is used by both the new right and neoconservatives to justify and preserve their privi-leged position in society. Neoliberals use the language of equity and democ-racy, creating a perception in society that they are working at narrowing the divide between socioeconomic classes. This rhetoric is yet another example of a color-blind ideology. It codes behaviorist language that has been associated with biological theories of intelligence while maintaining White racial hegemony.

Although antiracist projects are not widely accepted in education, the work of the advocates and scholars does give us hope that the field will and must expand. This expansion must include moving from what teachers *say they do* to what *they actually do*. It is critical to move teacher ideologies and subsequent pedagogies past perceived equity toward a realist view of how equitable teaching can be achieved. To counter White racial hegemony, we must begin documenting tangible outcomes of transformative professional development. And since antiracist professional development has historically focused on the rejection of White privilege, rather than transforming the political structures that reproduce it, we must move to an anti-White supremacist model if we are committed to RET. This will ground the field of transformative professional development in racial realism and give us tools to combat the structural components that work for the status quo: White supremacy. The need to commit ourselves to a racial realism ideology will support counterhegemonic educational political projects to achieve RET for our students.

Racially Equitable Teaching

I n 1981 James Banks began a movement to examine the social structures of schools from a multicultural perspective. He believed in "educational equality" for all students and used this theory as he conceptualized multicultural education. Banks (1981, 1989) held that a sustainable "multicultural school environment" could exist only when an entire school community was examined and transformed to include its policies, curriculum, assessment, and teachers' dispositions. Since then scholars have documented the effects of teaching and learning environments on students and we know that sustainable equity outcomes depend upon community collaboration (Comer, 1996) that challenges White, heterosexual, Eurocentric curricula that is used to distort the reality of the experiences of People of Color in the U.S. (Banks, 1993; Barba, Pang, & Tran, 1992; Janzen, 1994; McIntosh, 2000; Rist, 1991).

Practical strategies are missing from this body of literature, strategies that move teachers from a perception orientation to one of reality when discussing educational equity. It is well documented that most teachers work from a color-blind racial ideology, which is then translated into their pedagogies. And I have argued in Chapter III how these pedagogies are then supported through publicly funded professional development racial projects. Therefore, teacher ideology and professional development are central to issues of equity in schools. This question is very important for the application of practical classroom strategies: What is the relationship between these ideologies, pedagogies, professional development, and students? RET builds on the work of scholars in the fields of multicultural and antiracist education, critical race theory, Whiteness studies, and early childhood education to present a theory of teaching that will address this key question. The goals for RET are racial authenticity, racial balance, and positive racial in-group messaging and an effort to support teachers, administrators, community members, and public policymakers with tools to promote equitable learning environments for all students grounded in racial realism and supported through research. I present RET in three sections. The first section—"Racial Identity in Early Childhood"—will address the key issue of how teacher ideologies and pedagogies construct and deconstruct academic identities impacting student success in early childhood education. It is critical that we have a common understanding of the intimate connection between our own ideologies and how they impact student learning to begin a detailed discussion of RET. The second section—"Language, Thought, and Identity"—will present the assumptions and tenets that form the theoretical framework I use to justify and conceptualize RET and how these goals are intended to be interpreted by teachers, administrators, community members, and public policymakers. And the final section— "RET: Root Assumptions and Tenets"—will present how we can begin to assess if these goals are met in public educational settings.

Racial Identity in Early Childhood

Infants and toddlers are involved in self-awareness, possessing the ability to distinguish what "is me" from what "is not me." As they grow, they mimic adult behaviors, and by the age of two are aware of physical differences such as color. Preschoolers (three- to four-year-olds) can become confused with multiple classification systems (Asher & Allen, 1969; Burns, 1979; Harter, 1983; Ramsey, 1987; Spencer, 1985). Skin tone, hair texture, and eye shape are of great interest to children as they are discovering new observation skills. They believe that as their bodies grow, physical traits such as skin and hair color can change. For this reason, oversimplified racial grouping occurs. They will not have the ability to make multiple distinctions within racial groups until they are five or six years of age. These limited and often distorted thinking processes lead children to believe in stereotypes and form pre-prejudices, which is the beginning of racial awareness.

White-Biased Choice Behavior

Between the ages of three and six, both children of Color and White children historically have displayed White-biased choice behavior (Katz, 1987; McAdoo, 1985). Although current documentation shows that this trend is diminishing, Phyllis Katz (1987), director of the University of Colorado's Institute for Research on Social Problems at Boulder from 1975-1990, reports definite own-group preference in White children. And it has been proved both historically and currently that White children "often express negative comments toward other groups and never state a desire to be anything else but White" (pp. 93-94). Older children of Color who have achieved race consistency display same race preference while their White counterparts remain Eurocentric (Katz, 1987; McAdoo, 1985). Katz's research focus's on the importance of analyzing the interplay between gender, social class and race. In a longitudinal study on early predictors of children's intergroup attitudes conducted by Katz and Barrett (1997), they found that both gender and race could lead to biases in young children, which are then further effected by class, family and community.

> Children with high ingroup favoritism scores also had parents who were negative about racial diversity. For Whites, high ingoup favoritism was associated with parental beliefs that it was not important to talk about race. Black children with higher ingroup favoritism were more apt to speak about noticing racial differences than did Black children with lower scores (p.11).

Understanding that racial consistency is generally acquired by the age of seven or eight underscores the need for educators to interrupt these cycles of favoritism. Children of Color enter school with positive self-concepts (Holmes, 1995; McAdoo, 1985; Porter & Washington, 1989) yet are often perceived by teachers as having low self-esteem. It is only after a few years in school that they begin to self-doubt (Kunjunji, 1990; Persell, 1993). This is contrary to what the "early research⁹"–which was steeped in myth rather than empirical data and produced the deficit model of education that Martin Haberman (1990) presents in his pedagogy of poverty–shows. It is at this age that children are no longer confused with multiple classification systems, and realize that their skin, hair, and other physical characteristics will remain constant throughout their lives. They can view an individual as multidimensional, as discussed by Piaget. Due to this fact, individuals can be members of multiple groups simultaneously. Because they are leaving a predominantly egocentric stage of development, children have a greater capacity to empathize with individuals and groups. Recognizing that high-poverty schools have the largest concentration of students of Color, and that the disparity between students of Color and teachers of Color are greatest in these schools (*Assessment of Diversity in American's Teaching Workforce*, 2004, p. 5) dictates that White teachers have knowledge and skills to support this critical stage of identity development to counter the pedagogy of poverty currently accepted in urban and high –poverty schools districts.

Stereotyping and Identity Deconstruction

As children move from one-dimensional thinking and become adept at multiclassification systems, there is an increase in positive same-race identification (Doyle et al., 1988). Stereotyping is prevalent in preschool–a period of preoperations and the beginning of classification systems—peaks in kindergarten, and then drops when children are adept at multiple classification and multidimensional thinking. This leads to a "flexibility in beliefs" (Doyle et al., 1988), indicating the potential of children to critically analyze cultural and racial identity. In doing so, they are able to counter their differential treatment as a group and succeed through their own agency. Young people who receive what Sanders (1997) terms "positive racial socialization," Aboud and Doyle (1995) term "in-group pride" surpass those who do not on standard academic achievement measures in the U.S. Although this research may appear positive, it is in the analysis of the broader context that the problematic nature of the information becomes clear. In the early stages of identity construction, most children prefer Whiteness to Blackness (Hodge, Struckman, & Trost, 1975). This is a societal issue and not unique to any one racial group (Cross, 1991; Katz et al., 1987). In addition, those who receive what Witty and DeBaryshe (1994) term as "negative teacher interactions" are often the lowest achieving students.

As White children progress through kindergarten and then to a stage of abstract thinking with the ability to multiclassify, they have and continue to form their identity from the preferred status. Children of Color must work through White preference to a position when they will be able to accept and embrace their race. So, although stereotyping decreases, the positive Black identity associations are in response to negative associations. This is what I term identity deconstruction. White children do not have to form an identity in response to a racial deficit model. It is within this context that children construct individual and group identities. Skin color is not simply an outward, easily recognizable characteristic but a defining factor (Cross, 1985; Semaj, 1985; Spencer, 1982, 1984, 1985). And although much of the research in early childhood racial identity has centered on a Black/White American binary, it can be applied to all People of Color through Cross' "bicultural competency" model. Cross (1991) presents how Black children as young as three can be biculturally competent, understanding and embodying differential treatment based on race.[10] An argument would be that this competency can then be applied to all areas of identity construction and all racial groups in early childhood.

Pioneering developmentalists Corsaro and Miller (1992) argue for greater attention to be given to sociocultural context and its impact on collective and interpretive reproduction in identity construction. This does not negate the importance of cognitive theory; rather it clarifies the limitations and builds on the useful aspects of these studies. One aspect of sociocultural context is collective and interpretive reproduction theory. It recognizes that children are actors and constructors of socially mediated knowledge. Paul Connolly addresses this and reports in his 1998 study *Racism, Gender Identities and Young Children*, children "appropriate, rework and reproduce discourses on race, gender and sexuality in quite complex ways" (p. 187) as they construct and socially mediate knowledge. This places identity construction within a framework that examines language acquisition and concept formation through discourse. Van Ausdale and Feagin (2001) bridge the cognitive and sociocultural theorists in *The First R: How Children Learn Race and Racism* (2001). Their research finds that "the language and ideas of race empower White children to set themselves apart as 'better' than racialized others, and by so doing they learn and perform the practices associated with being 'white American'" (p. 34). The works of Corsaro and Miller, Connolly, and Van Ausdale and Feagin clearly support that language acquired, discourse entered, and actions applied in cultural contexts impact our concept formation, shaping identities in early childhood.

Language, Thought, and Identity

Vygotsky (1978) states that (1) human development and learning occur as a result of an individual's interaction with society and (2) this interaction takes place in and is informed by a particular cultural context. One can make sense of their world through dialogue and direct applications of solutions and personal theories each has in their environment. This leads to socially constructed and contextually bound knowledge. These interactions "scaffold" (build and join together in organizational models that have direct relevance to the learner) through classroom interactions with teachers and peers to acquire and accommodate new knowledge. Scaffolding happens during the zone of proximal development (ZPD).

Vygotsky (1962, 1986) explains that the language and speech of adults attributes meanings to words and sounds and it is through these verbal communications that adults are able to predetermine the development of a child's generalizations to its final destination—a fully formed concept (pp. 120-122). Generalizations and categories are determined when children form complexes. A complex is the union of subjective impressions and bonds that exist between objects. Bonds are concrete and factual and discovered by the learner through direct or scientifically developed experience (pp. 122-123). The bridge between complexes and concept formation is the pseudo-concept, which is a spontaneously developed complex by the child as it moves toward concept formation (pp. 188-120). This exemplifies how language acquired in schools through interactions with adults and older peers creates concepts that become thoughts acted upon and embodied by children in their developing identities.

Embodiment of Conceptual Metaphors

Vygotsky states (1986), "An analysis of the interaction of thought and word must begin with an investigation of the different phases and planes, a thought transverses before it is embodied in words." (p. 218) In other words, we are seeking out the sociocultural history of a particular thought to understand the relationship between semantics and event knowledge. Foucault expands this work when he discusses "the history of systems of thought" that creates norms in society that are then embodied by the participants. These norms, or functional embodiments, are "used automatically, unconsciously and without noticeable effort" (Lakoff, 1987, p. 12). Discourse between adults and children produce generalizations and categories, leading to concepts and then norms, which become embodied in conceptual metaphors informing our discourse.

Lakoff and Johnson (1980) address the importance of metaphors as applied to identity when they state,

> Just as we seek out metaphors to highlight and make coherent what we have in common with someone else, we also seek out personal metaphors to highlight and make coherent our own pasts, our present activities, and our dreams, hopes, and goals as well. (pp. 222-223)

Metaphors allow an individual or group to communicate ideas, which are not known or understood, to another individual or group. Metaphors are used for concept–meaning making. They structure what we do and how we understand what we are doing. "The most fundamental values in a culture will be coherent with the metaphorical structure of the most fundamental concepts in the culture" (p. 22). Values embedded within a culture are therefore embedded within the metaphors they construct and use, "since cultural understanding underlies metaphor usage" (Quinn, 1991).

This underscores the importance of the language exchanges between young children and their adult world. The adults are passing on language that is context-specific, dependent upon the "schooling"[11] and sociocultural experiences they have had. How the adults in their environment identify themselves and others will become part of the complexes that will lead to concept formation in children. Just as experience incites the construction of complexes, it also expands conceptual metaphor construction. Having "critical"[12] and diverse sociocultural experiences supports the growth of our language and thinking. This in turn gives us a richness of knowledge to draw upon when the metaphors embedded in our language create dissonance within our concept of identity and do not promote "coherence" (Colby, 1991). Colby explains that in the process of coherence, an individual transforms or transcends a "state" where he/she feels inadequate.

Scholars of race have a long history of applying racial metaphor to address "the human condition" of racism. Bell created for himself an image when he published *Faces at the Bottom of the Well: The Permanence of Racism* (1992); Mills clearly addressed in *The Racial Contract* (1999) the legal structures that serve to stratify society by race; and Anzaldua's *Borderlands* (1987) presented the psychological, political, and physical territoriality of race thorough the internalization of borders. Morrison in *Dancing in the Dark: Whiteness and Literary Imagination* (1993) deconstructs dominant literary metaphors (and ensuing concepts formed in response to their use) in American society. When discussing what the term American means today, she concludes, "Race, in fact, now functions as a metaphor so necessary to the construction of Americanness that it rivals the old pseudo-scientific and class-informed racisms whose dynamics we are more used to deciphering" (p. 47).

Each of these scholars took a form of language—metaphor—and used it as a powerful tool for bridging gaps between what one sees, embodies, and lives within racial realism. Metaphor in each of these cases has had the power to transform thinking, and as such, they serve as examples of how prevalent and embedded they are in society.

The White Knight

What do racial metaphors look like in early childhood classrooms? As a former kindergarten, elementary, and middle school teacher, I witnessed many examples of how these racial metaphors are applied by young children and young adults. Here I recount an incident that took place in the dramatic play area of my classroom.

Every day Caden and Terrance began their day in drama reading books and creating plays, a pattern they had developed and enjoyed. They entered kindergarten not knowing each other; soon they found that they shared a love of reading and a large vocabulary. They were immensely interested in finding new words, investigating their meanings, and took great pride in writing. They were drawn to each other and soon became close friends. Both were avid readers and shared a love and fascination for King Arthur and his Knights. The boys would regulary take on character roles and retell their favorite stories. After about two months Terrance became withdrawn. I was perplexed at this and observed that he no longer would read in the class library, a favorite area of our room, and he played in isolation, often subdued and openly depressed.

Caden missed Terrance, and discussed this with other students and me. Terrance's mother noticed this behavior too when she dropped him at school and she too was concerned. Caden called a class meeting, a right a student of K-7 can exercise. He followed a model all knew well. He would state his problem or concern; anyone involved in the problem would respond and they could have questions and comments from three classmates before setting an action plan. Caden announced, "I miss Terrance, he is my best friend and he will not play with me anymore, I want him back." Terrance sat with his head down staring at the rug in our class meeting area. His shoulders shrugged and for a moment I did not believe he would respond. Finally and with great purpose Terrance raised his head and looked squarely at Caden, "You said I had to be the Black Knight!" "But you're Black, Terrance, and I am White, so you should be the Black Knight," replied Caden. "I don't want to be the Black Knight, he's BAD!" stated Terrance emphatically. (Earick, 1997)

Each of the boys believed their position was important enough to defend and I, as an educator, knew it was my responsibility to assist them as they deconstructed this metaphor and moved toward a new concept of what the "Black Knight" constituted. We held a class meeting, each boy stated his position, requested comments or questions, clarified issues of concern to the class, and finally came to a conclusion. We agreed that the Black Knight "didn't have to be bad" and that whoever decided to take on a role would be in charge of telling the group "who they were and how they play." In addition, I was given the responsibility of finding books that had characters that look like Terrance and portrayed Black Knights as "good" people, and if I could not find them I had to make them. We went on to research authentic publishers of Black and African American children's literature and we also put on display several class books. Terrance approved of our work and became an active participant and leader in our classroom once again.

Without the intervention of a class meeting, a positive complex would have been attached to the "White Knight," contributing to a race-positive pseudo-complex formation, while a negative complex would have been attached to the "Black Knight," contributing to a race-negative pseudo-complex formation. This had the potential to affect how Caden and Terrance viewed themselves racially since the social climate in the classroom would have supported the conceptual metaphors "White is good" and "Black is bad" if this intervention had not occurred.

The pervasiveness of a negative association coupled with the word Black and positive association coupled with the word White is embedded in our everyday language and demonstrated by the seemingly innocent act of looking up a definition in a dictionary,[13] something teachers do regularly in the classroom (see Table 4).

Table 4: Conceptual Metaphors in Standard English Dictionaries			
Main Entry Definitions	Conceptual Metaphor	Main Entry Definitions	Conceptual Metaphor
BLACK	BLACK IS BAD	WHITE	WHITE IS GOOD
Indicative of condemnation or discredit	Black mark	Marked by upright fairness	That's mighty White of you
Of or relating to covert intelligence operations	Black government programs	Instigated or carried out by reactionary forces as a counterrevolutionary measure	A White terror
Dirty, soiled	Hands, black with grime	Free from spot or blemish	White
Of the color black	His face was black with rage	Of the color white	White with fear
Connected with or invoking the supernatural and especially the devil	Black magic	Not intended to cause harm	White magic
Marked by the occurrence of disaster	Black Friday	Marked by the wearing of white by the woman as a symbol of purity	White wedding
Characterized by hostility or angry discontent	Black resentment filled his heart	Passionate	White fury
Characterized by grim, distorted, or grotesque satire	Black comedy	Pale gray; silvery and lustrous	White hair
Characterized by the absence of light	Black night	Favorable, fortunate	White days

Metaphor and Race Consistency

As mentioned earlier, racial consistency generally occurs between the ages of seven and eight. The complexes and pseudo-complexes created at this stage of development become the language and thought base from which one makes sense of the self. Conceptual metaphors, as described earlier, are embedded within this language delivered to the child from the adults within the environment, as illustrated in Table 4. Therefore, the content and messages embedded within conceptual metaphors work to construct identities.

The conceptual metaphors "White is good" and "Black is bad" exemplify the embedded messages children are exposed to during the sensitive stage of race consistency, which impacts their racial identity construction/deconstruction. Young children need exposure to alternative metaphors that embed positive and egalitarian views of their race and promote positions of power fostering positive in-group messages. Teachers have the potential to use language and discourse in strategic ways to fairly and equally support students through the construction of positive in-group messages and affirming identities.

When we allow racialized language to overprivilege White students, our reality as Whites becomes one of misrepresentation and self-deception. Concept and complex formation based on misrepresentations and self-deception supports a White reality of the natural order and the right to "conquest, colonize and enslave" (Spring, 1998, p. 19). Concept and complex formation (Vygotsky, 1986, pp. 112-113) construct coded language networks that inform identity in early childhood and are perpetuated through sociocultural interactions with the adults in our environment. In this manner, White supremacy is perpetuated through an efficient, systematic indoctrination process that is based on a false collective memory, which Corrigan and Derek (1985) present as an inseparable and active organization of forgetting that, I now argue, becomes reality to the young learner.

Learning Race and Racism

I have discussed the racialized nature of urban schools' standard measures of success through the achievement gap, teacher workforce, and the progression of identity construction in early childhood. In each case I stressed the social context as the catalyst for racialized behavior. In the field of early childhood education, research has applied predominantly discrete measures, many based on forced choice tests and short-term interviews. This information, although valuable, is at the same time limiting because of its narrow focus. Therefore, more in-depth and comprehensive work is needed to fully support the competencies I have outlined in racial identity formation in early childhood.

The recent ethnographic study conducted by sociologists Van Ausdale and Joe Feagin in their book *The First R: How Children Learn Race and Racism* (2001), is the first in-depth and comprehensive work that bridges social cognition and racism in early childhood education. They spent a year in a multiracial preschool observing three- and four-year-olds making sense of race through their everyday experiences. They found a social and cultural structure of racialized language, concepts, practices, and role expectation within which children operate (p. 34) when making sense of their racial roles. These roles are the mechanisms through which young children in schools "learn and use ideas about race and ethnicity" that become embedded "in their everyday language and practice of identities" (p. 33). Racial identities (as well as gendered, sexed, and linguistic) are made concrete and normalized through privileges and disadvantages. These norms are then perceived as truths by the adults and peer in the school or internalized and embodied by the students through an indoctrination process.

In their research, Van Ausdale and Feagin have identified four dimensions of racial and ethnic relations that the young children they worked with experienced, what they say might be called the "racializing process." They are (1) concepts and thinking; (2) spoken discourse; (3) everyday practices and performances that restrict or privilege; (4) identities and psychological (and physical) embodiment—all of which happen during social interactions in the school with peers and adults. Key findings in their research are discussed in Chapter XI and include the following:

1. Children quickly learn the racial-ethnic identities and role performances of the larger society (p.182);
2. They take on the language and concepts of the larger society and experiment with them in their own interactions with other children and adults (p.182);
3. Categorizations such as "Black" or white are socially reoccurring and shape the social interactions in which each child and adult participates (p. 184);
4. Children are neither naive nor color-blind; race and ethnic relationships are important aspects of their social world (p.190);
5. The perception that children are racially naive is a construction of white adults (p191);
6. Children as young as three and four understand racial-ethnic relations (p.196).

Van Ausdale and Feagin conclude, "When the nature of everyday discourse and practice is laden with racial-ethnic meanings, children, too, will make much practical use of that discourse" (p. 198).

A Threat in the Air: How Stereotypes Shape Academic Identity and Performance

The implications of Van Ausdale and Feagin's work can be seen in Steele's research in stereotype threat. Steele (1997) explains that it is a "situational threat—a threat in the air—that, in general form, can affect the members of any group about whom a negative stereotype exists. Where bad stereotypes about these groups apply, members of these groups can fear being reduced to that stereotype" (p. 614). In academic settings this translates into students who identify as high achieving from an early age and continue to do so until a "situational threat" is introduced, and those who identify as low achieving and continue to do so until the cycle is intentionally disrupted.

Steele proposes "wise schools" (p. 624) as one way to disrupt situational stereotypes. These schools actively work toward securing "students in the belief that they will not be held under the suspicion of negative stereotypes about their group." Steele cites the work of Comer (1988) and the School Development Program in New Haven, CT, as an early childhood location that has seen great success in applying this strategy. As a fellow in the School Development Program I was trained by Dr. Comer[14] and his associates over a three-year period in the deconstruction of racial, gender, sexed, and linguistic stereotypes through community-based schools and teacher self-reflection. Its effects could be transformative if the majority of the teachers who attended the program work as a collective to understand and interrupt the overprivileging and disprivileging stereotypes in their day-to-day lives.

The work of Van Ausdale and Feagin (2001) supports the importance of language acquisition and application, identifying concepts, thinking, and discourse as defining factors in our identity construction. Metaphors and situational threats work as language projects that produce psychological and physical outcomes in the form of embodiment. Teacher pedagogies apply and use racially coded language in the form of assimilation and tolerance to rearticulate a White supremacist social order.

Identity is constructed and deconstructed through the interactions and relationships formed within our sociocultural context. This context decides how and if we are allowed to access identity information to form positive in-group concepts, how we accommodate this knowledge, and later apply it consciously and unconsciously in our environment. It is well documented that teachers hold lower expectations for students of Color and higher expectations for White students (Murray & Jackson, 1999). Consequently, teacher expectations based on racial groupings of students become self-fulfilling (Persell, 1993). This becomes clear as we come to find that students who have had a teacher of their own race, on average, score 3 to 4 percentile points higher on standardized tests of reading and math than peers who had teachers of different races (Dee, 2001). Most importantly, this effect is cumulative, increasing every year a student had a same-race teacher. Early childhood teachers are White and the majority are women, who teach from a White, female, middle-class perspective that has been shown to alienate students of color (Gay, 1993). This creates a social context privileging identities of White students as high performers and students of Color as low performers, establishing racialized norms of success that is supported through White hegemonic curriculum and professional development.

As stated earlier, Blau (2003) concludes, after analyzing ten years of two data sets from the Department of Education's National Center for Educational Statistics, that "The best single indicator of children's vulnerability (in school) is the color of their skin" (p. 203), with Whites being the criterion group for all measures of success. If we allow our students to enter educational systems that predetermine success and failure based on race, we are normalizing a White identity of high performance and an identity of low performance for People of Color. Not only are 90% of our teachers White but also alarmingly 40% of our schools have no teachers of Color (NCES, 2004). This further awards unfair advantages to White students, who make up 60% of the school community, while dismissing the long-term effects racial stratification has on students of Colors. For these reasons, I privilege race as a defining factor in our developing identities, which are mediated by classroom artifacts and teacher ideologies in the form of applied pedagogies. Race matters in schools and teachers must begin the process of deconstructing their racial ideologies to promote equitable classrooms.

History has shaped and informed our thinking as collective racial groups; significance of our ancestry and heritage must be acknowledged. In this manner we become cognizant of our responsibility as dominant or subordinate members of society. In addition, we need to become aware of our multiple positions as an oppressor and the oppressed (Freire, 2000). Accepting how Whites systematically benefit from all other communities through oppressive norms in our educational system is the foundation of racial identity construction/deconstruction, which informs RET. The language, texts, and images applied and mediated in the classroom adds to collective thinking. This thinking works toward either positive or negative in-group identity messages. The relationship between language acquisition and identity construction is critical during sensitive periods of growth and development. Early childhood is such a period. The construction of positive and equitable identities is a precursor to academic and social success. Unfortunately, few White educators in early childhood have been exposed to theory and research in the area of identity construction/deconstruction, and more specifically, racial identity, to understand their position of power and authority over collective and internalized identities. White early childhood educators must change this trend in teacher preparation programs to support an egalitarian educational system and society.

The possibility lies within each of us to emancipate ourselves from White power and privilege through the application of transformative pedagogies grounded in racial realism.

For White teachers to be able to internalize this research and apply it in their classrooms, they must first identify their own racial ideologies. Then they will have the ability to see how it is manifested in their pedagogies through language, image, and text artifacts in their classrooms. How these ideologies shape and inform racially equitable professional development projects will be an important finding for future work in this field because it will give designers of future projects insights into how teachers can transform pedagogies to promote social justice through RET in their classrooms.

RET: Root Assumptions and Tenets

There are three root assumptions to RET: (1) White racial hegemony perpetuates White supremacy in our educational system; (2) White racial hegemony is reproduced through publicly funded professional development; (3) teacher pedagogies construct and deconstruct racial identities in academic settings based on a White-based norm. We know that all forms of oppression including racism work on institutional, cultural, and individual levels; therefore, the tenets of RET cannot simply be adopted by one teacher or classroom but must ultimately become an integral part of teacher education and professional development at every level to include universities, colleges, and classrooms if our goal is to close the achievement gap. I have established how White racial hegemony perpetuates White supremacy in our educational system and how White racial hegemony is reproduced through publicly funded professional development. Now that we understand the serious nature of racial identity development in academic settings, I can define the tenets of RET.

I will present the tenets according to three expectations that align with RET's root assumptions. They are to (1) challenge Eurocentric curriculum and teaching materials; (2) expect racially equitable academic identity development; and (3) dedicate professional development funds to support RET projects.

Table 5: Tenets of RET—Expectation 1
Expectation 1: Challenge Eurocentric Curriculum and Teaching Materials
Diverse racial perspectives are presented and assessed according to their impact on an equitable society.
No one racial group dominates in image, text, and classroom discourse.

We know that the majority of curriculum and teaching materials are White, Eurocentric, and heterosexual male centered. And we know that children as young as three apply knowledge from these materials in their play, taking on roles and acting out socially constructed norms in an effort to clarify their position in society. In addition, we know that not all perspectives are equal, therefore, we must ask ourselves: are our perspectives grounded in actions that are dominating or emancipating people? When Caden insisted that Terrance must be the Black Knight by virtue of his skin color, he was dictating Terrance's identity, dominating him. Caden was confident in his conviction that this was normal and expected behavior in society. His conviction was based on images and stories he has seen and heard on a regular and ongoing basis in books, cartoons, and television, which has informed what he now interprets as truth and knowledge. Because White heterosexual males are privileged in each of the media, Caden has not gained insights into alternative perspectives; he is being indoctrinated into White racial hegemony and working to do the same to Terrance. One might ask why a child so young, five years of age, would dominate. We know that children want to define who they are and what they have control over; it gives them security and a sense of place. For Caden, adopting these views on race gave him great power. He knew he would always have the preferred role in their acting, that of the hero. The hero supports the perception of honor, goodness, and intelligence, while the Black Knight was the villain, supporting the perception of deviance and unintelligence.

Deviance has been historically associated with domination. Women who participated in nonmarital sex were historically considered deviant until the women's rights movement; Blacks and African Americans are portrayed as having deviant traits such as gang membership, drug abuse, and promiscuity; Indigenous Peoples are associated with alcoholism and gambling; gays and lesbians are associated with deteriorating mental and physical health. And just as Caden insisted that Terrance play the Black Knight, these deviant roles are expected and normalized as group racial behaviors through print and image media. We translate these roles into the metaphors we apply in our language that inform the complexes our thinking processes draw upon each day. In academic settings, these interactions are based on curriculum used in classrooms. Therefore, schools are the gatekeepers of knowledge production and as such can balance the perspectives presented by not allowing any one group to dominate text, image, or classroom discourse. Children of Color, such as Terrance, know from experience that he or she will have to challenge negative views associated with his or her identity that was based on race, as Terrance did with Caden in my class. It is critical to assist White children as they begin to identify as a community member, rather than oppressor.

Table 6: Tenets of RET—Expectation 2
Expectation 2: Support Racially Equitable Academic Identity Development
Cycles of racism to include negative in-group messages and stereotype threat are interrupted and never accepted
Students receive racially balanced positive in-group messaging
Student and family voices of diverse racial heritage are honored and represented in classrooms, school, and district policymaking

In-group messages are communicated daily through curriculum and teaching materials presented in classrooms. We know that these in-group messages work to construct or deconstruct academic identities in schools and that they have the capacity to be associated with gendered, sexed, and raced groups of children, manifesting themselves in stereotype threat. We know the majority of these materials privilege Whites, in particular White heterosexual males. Therefore, just as curriculum and teaching materials are controlled and manipulated by educational gatekeepers, so are racial identities in academic settings.

During a lesson on the Pueblo Revolt in a New Mexico public school, I observed a young student, Thomas, present to his teacher his family's perspective on this historical event. Thomas explained how his grandparents and their ancestors who lived on the Pueblo had an account that was not in the textbook, that of domination and stolen lands. His teacher interrupted his account, which had every student's attention, and said, "That is a very interesting thought and I think I know where you are going with this, just trust me and I'll get to it." Thomas respectfully did as he was told and appeared to believe his teacher. I observed all three lessons on the Revolt and the teacher never made any mention of Indigenous Peoples or that their lands were taken and peoples murdered; he presented explorers and immigrants as intelligent, brave, and forward-thinking individuals. He gave an account of his own family members from the time of their immigration from Germany to the period when his grandfather became a nationally known scientist: a fact he presented with great pride and he felt he had communicated to his students the importance of exploration and immigration in recent history. I watched Thomas become more withdrawn over the next three days and disappointed;

he had trusted that his teacher would address the perspectives on this event with respect and accuracy, and instead Thomas' perspectives were deemed invisible. We know that invisibility is often the method Whites use in classrooms to deal with the history of Indigenous Peoples. So, in addition to navigating White curriculum, which portrays Indigenous Peoples as savage simpletons, Thomas now had to navigate becoming invisible in a classroom where it was believed he had the opportunity to share his authentic and accurate family history. The views of Thomas, his grandparents, and their ancestors had no place there.

The interaction I observed and documented in the classroom is consistent with the majority of observations I have made over five years in supervisory positions in New Mexico of White teachers presenting American history. In addition, this teacher and many others in New Mexico communicated to me that their texts were culturally relevant, free of stereotypes, and present accurate information concerning Indigenous peoples. This was largely based on the fact that the word savage was omitted from the texts. No other rationale was offered. Teachers were told by their district officer and school principal that their texts were culturally relevant and the teacher accepted this as fact, communicating to me their deskilling (Apple, 1996) in a very tangible manner.

Positive racial in-group messaging is not only communicated through curriculum and classroom discourse, it is also informed by community relationships. These relationships begin between policymakers and school districts, directly affecting schools, teachers, and families through mandates. These mandates, made by educational policymakers, are politically and historically supported by dominant ideology, which in the U.S. is White racial hegemony. This increases positive White in-group messaging and has lasting effects on academic identities that impact how they test on standard measures of success currently in our public schools. This communicates the critical need to expect at all times that positive in-group messaging applies to all levels of education and to all raced peoples in a balanced and equitable manner.

Table 7: Tenets of RET–Expectation 3
Expectation 3: Dedicates Professional Development Funds to Support RET
Authentic scholars, administrators, and practitioners present on topics pertaining to their own race
Alliances are created with outside agencies to identify racially authentic resources for classroom teachers
Colleagues meet, listen and discuss critical racial incidents on a regular and ongoing basis

To close the achievement gap, educators must gain the skills needed to apply RET. Dedicated professional development must be allotted for this purpose. This makes sense when all political parties espouse the need for equity in educational outcomes, high standards, and accountability. If our government believes in educational equity, then it needs to look at the reality of race. This can be accomplished by drawing on over thirty years of research by racially authentic scholars I have presented. Their work has documented the relationship between race, academic identities, and the achievement gap in the U.S. Ignoring their collective expertise and knowledge is one more example of a color-blind ideology. This incident of color blindness targets the youngest and most susceptible to abuse in our society, our children. Therefore, policymakers, administrators, and educators who continue to ignore the work of authentic scholars in early childhood education are engaging in a structural form of child abuse. To stop this abuse, alliances must be created between community members and outside agencies that can assist with the identification of racially authentic resources and mentorship in their use by classroom teachers.

We know that White teacher dispositions are grounded in color blindness, and even those who categorize themselves as being aware of race have had virtually no coursework in the identification of their own racial ideologies, how these are manifested through artifacts in their classrooms, and the impact they have on the construction or deconstruction of academic identities based on race. Admitting our ignorance as White educators, scholars, and policymakers allows us to identify where we need change, something we constantly emphasize to children in classrooms. Keeping and discussing critical racial incidents in our educational settings focuses teachers on what they are doing rather than what they perceive they are doing and becomes the self-reflective component to RET. Once authentic scholars, administrators, and practitioners provide us with racially authentic research and pedagogy, methods, and alliances are formed to identify and mentor teachers in the use of racially authentic materials, teachers can self-reflect personally and collectively through the use of critical incidents based on race.

Goals

The goals of RET are to present racial authenticity, racial balance, and positive racial in-group messaging to students through school curriculum and community relationships, regardless of the racial make-up of a school. These goals, if applied and practiced on all levels of education from universities to classrooms, will shift market demand of curricula from the current White heterosexual European male focus to racially authentic, balanced curriculum materials that present positive in-group messaging for dominant and nondominant peoples. This shift in knowledge production holds the potential to support equitable academic identities in our schools, one way to work toward social justice.

Racial Authenticity

Central to a White supremacist ideology is the disregard for knowledge produced both historically and currently by People of Color. Therefore, maintaining racially authentic texts, images, and discourse written by diverse People of Color grounded in racial realism counters White racial hegemony by offering alternative perspectives to current curriculums.

Racial Balance

As seen in the far right's White national separatist movement and the new right's use of racial-based fear tactics, racial isolation and distorted media images promote and perpetuate White supremacy. Expecting that all classrooms present curriculum materials that reflect the natural diversity of our country becomes a practical way to ensure all students begin a process of positive messaging for racial groups other than their own.

Positive Racial In-Group Messaging

We know that in-group messaging has effects on all members of a group. Shifting our attention from individual to collective interactions will allow us to assess and balance the levels of privilege, support, and compliments we offer various racial groups during teaching.

Evaluation

Evaluation of RET must be grounded in authentic practice and racial realism that supports transformative pedagogies. Therefore, each teacher is an action researcher and inventories text and image artifacts each year to hone their skills in balancing racially authentic materials. They keep critical racial incident logs to see how children make sense of their racial identities in school settings while participating in discourse inquiry to see how they make sense of their racial identities. In addition, through a timed interval analysis of a taped lesson, teachers are able to code the in-group messaging communicated through teacher-students interactions and student-student interactions. One method of reflecting on in-group messaging is the assessment of dominant Curriculum Discourse Phases (CDP), Discourse Skills Development (DSD), and power contexts applied in the classroom through teacher-student in-group messaging. I have applied each of these to a Racial Discourse Observation Protocol for Teacher Self Reflection (see Appendix A). Teachers can then reflect upon tangible behaviors they exhibit that impact their pedagogies, using the protocol to increase their ability to attain RET goals.

CDP

"Interactive Phases of Curricular and Personal Revision with Regard to Race" originated from McIntosh's (1990) study with faculty of the department of women's studies at Wellesley. Her work on White privilege led to a review of the process as a racial event. She has applied it in the assessment of "patterns management, leadership, government, science and social government policy, education and interpersonal behavior" (p. 6). And she argues that it is a reliable tool to use in programs that stress changing thoughts and practices. These phases focus analysis of curriculum as racialized discourses.

Phase I	All-White history
Phase II	Exceptional minority individuals
Phase III	Minority issues, minority groups as problems, anomalies, absences, or victims
Phase IV	The lives and cultures of people of Color everywhere as history
Phase V	History redefined and reconstructed to include all

The goal for teachers is to move through the phases until they can present at Phase V on a regular basis. It works to dismantle the White, heterosexual, Eurocentric male curriculum focus that currently dominates education.

DSD

DSD are discrete skills grounded in early childhood discourse skills acquisition that support academic empowerment and privilege in schools (see Pan & Snow, 1999; Schley & Snow, 1992; Snow & Tabors, 1993) through adult-student and student-adult language events. Pan and Snow (1999) outline the need for children to have the following cognitive and linguistic skills in order to "tell stories, make arguments, give explanations, provide definitions, or tell jokes" (p.237),

1. They must be able to take the listener's perspective into account
2. They must be able to express their own perspective
3. They must be able to take and signal alternative stances towards the information to be conveyed
4. They must master the conventions of different genres of discourse

These skills are modeled and practiced not only by peers but the adults in their environments. The skills can act as language artifacts that we code and reflect upon in our teaching pedagogies, striving to have all students relate knowledge to themselves and those around them regularly in multiple phases.

Discourse Building
Phase I	Describe: Give account of attributes
Phase II	Extend: Increasing an account of attributes
Phase III	Question: Posing doubt or uncertainty for clarification
Phase IV	Evaluate: Judge quality, value, or importance
Phase V	Challenge Demand an explanation, justification, or proof
Phase VI	Relate: Significant connection to one's lived experience

What level of critical thinking are students being asked to engage in? Are we expecting academic or social knowledge to be communicated and whose perspective is privileged? Each of these questions demand analysis of the skills of discourse we deliver in classrooms. We know that language events support concept formation (Vygotsky, 1986), metaphor acquisition (Lakoff, 1987; Lakoff & Johnson, 1980), and social construction of racial identities (Connolly, 1998; Van Ausdale & Feagin, 2001). We also know that these language events deliver in-group messages to children that inform their academic identities. This mandates that we critically explore qualitative and quantitative relationship between discourse, curriculum, White racial hegemony as we mentor teachers in how to support RET in our schools. Now the question is, what does RET look like?

• C H A P T E R   5 •

Organizing a Project

Issues of race and its study have a history of making White teachers "uncomfortable" (hooks, 1994, p. 39), and they can resist participation
through passive reactions even after consenting to participate. For White
teachers and educators, "[t]hinking about race becomes a highly charged emotional experience resulting in resistance, misunderstanding, rage and/or feelings of inefficacy" (Tatum, 1994 as quoted in Rosenberg, 2004, p. 259). I
spent four years observing and talking with teachers in Connecticut and New
Mexico about race and student achievement prior to designing ECRIE. In addition, I supervised student teachers and mentored teachers in a multilingual
literacy development projects as I applied components of what would become
ECRIE. And finally I modified components of ECRIE for inclusion in preservice teacher programs in New Mexico and South Carolina.

In each situation I collaborated with participants to understand their individual and collective needs in connection with the needs of their students,
reflecting on their personal stories and continually reevaluating the structures
in place that empowered dominant groups while regulating nondominant
groups. This process gave me insights into my own motivations for designing
this project. As I entered into conversations with teachers I found myself sharing my frustrations over the lack of information I was given on the role my
racial ideologies had on my students and my belief that if we all were offered
this research and theory in our preservice programs it would have changed
how we taught. In addition, I believed that if we wanted our profession to
progress we needed to find ways to change this and be accountable. I shared
stories of the racist texts and images I used in my own classroom over sixteen
years, unaware of their messages due to my own indoctrination into Whiteness. I later found out that these informal and often brief, interchanges were
the cause behind the teachers' staying in the projects. As one teacher said,
"they speak to your authenticity," referring to one of the three goals of RET

that we were exploring and discussing. The most notable outcome of these conversations was the recognition that all the teachers I worked with had little to no understanding of their own racial ideologies or how children form racial identities. They had immense potential to discuss their beliefs around gender, class, and to some degree language identities, yet when it came to race they were distressed. During our discussions on racial identity, they often responded by saying, "There is no racism in my class"; "I don't believe in racism"; or "Racism isn't an identity." Teachers consistently substituted "racism" for "racial" early in our conversations around identity and ideology, displaying their discomfort. However, over time they became interested in the topic and found reflecting on the interconnection between their racial ideologies, pedagogies, and how they are manifested in classroom artifacts empowering. I realized that to succeed I needed to interweave a professional development design that took into account White racial hegemony as applied in early childhood classrooms. This led to a focus on White teacher dispositions, to include ideology, race, and pedagogy. What emerged was a call for transformative professional development grounded in antiracism.

Planning and Design

The first step to successful professional development design is to understand what has and has not worked. Richardson and Anders (2005), researchers in the field of teacher professional development, literacy, and urban schools conclude, "beliefs that teacher participants bring into the program with them can block or enable learning" (p. 215). Professional development research has found that changing beliefs involves several components: (1) the use of practical arguments (Anders & Richardson, 1991; Fenstermacher, 1994); (2) dialogue (Wilson & Berne, 1999); (3) teacher-generated "texts" (or artifacts) as the base of inquiry (Ortiz, 2001) and small-scale studies that have shown potential; (4) facilitators as agents of change (Anders & Richardson, 1991; Grossman, Wineburg, & Woolworth, 2001; Ortiz, 2001). Professional development that stressed these four components successfully assisted teachers in changing beliefs and pedagogy in contrast to top-down models that have been shown to cause misunderstandings, discouragement, and a general sense of devaluing in the teaching profession (Peck, 2003). Education and literacy development scholars Richardson and Anders (2005) identify four key factors to consider in any professional development project (pp. 206-209):

1. The goals: Are they mandated or voluntary?
2. The agency of the participants: Do they have the opportunity to determine processes in the project?
3. The nature of the process: Does it match the goals?
4. What teachers will learn: Is it stressing content, activities, or processes?

The ideal is for a collective of teachers from a common school, content area, or grade level to unite over an extended period of time with a common purpose, supported with rich content, an outside facilitator, activities, and an authentic context to investigate a problem (Garet, Porter, Desimone, Birman, & Yoon, 2001).

We must also move away from workshop models of professional development, because we know they do not work in cases of effecting long-term change. Smylie's 1988 survey of teachers ranked district-organized workshops as the lowest choice and learning by experience in the classroom as the highest choice in learning opportunities in professional development. These preferences articulated by teachers are supported in the research, underscoring the importance of equity-based, active, context-rich learning environments for teachers and students to increase educational outcomes. This translates into a need to plan and design equity-based, content-rich, process-driven professional development to change teacher practices. Changing beliefs (Richardson, 2003; Richardson & Anders, 2005) is the first step in changing classroom practices and allowing teachers to become content (Brophy & Good, 1986; Gage, 1978; Good & Grouws, 1979; Stallings, Needels, & Stayrook, 1980; Anders & Richardson, 1991; Fenstermacher, 1994; Ortiz, 2001; Wilson & Berne, 1999) and process competent.

A clear sense of how the community is related to changes in teacher practices and beliefs is missing from the professional development research. Studies have suggested that an important element of successful projects (Garet et al., 2001; Palincsar, et al., 1998) is the participation of teachers in communities consisting of colleagues and administrators; little value is given to the students and their families as information resources. The role schools assign to families in education is what they can do for teachers to support student-learning outcomes. Missing are the political and equity resources families have to offer the educational communities to support student-learning outcomes.

It has been stated that changing teacher beliefs is critical for increasing observable student and teacher outcomes in content knowledge; yet what of context? What of the beliefs teachers hold of urban youth as low achievers, uninterested in education, and in control of their nonadvancement (Delpit, 1995; Kohn, 1998; Perry, 2002; Steele, 2003; Suarez-Orozco, 2002; Valdez,

1996)? It is in the relationship between ideological differences of schools, practitioners, and families that RET projects such as ECRIE hold great promise while applying the effective strategies used in schools to date: (1) the use of practical arguments; (2) dialogue; (3) teacher-generated "texts" *or artifacts*; and (4) facilitators as agents of change (see Table 8).

Table 8: ECRIE Alignment to Effective Professional Development

Effective Professional Development	ECRIE Professional Development
Practical Arguments	Equitable Student Outcomes
Dialogue	Action Model–Inquiry Groups
Teacher-Generated Texts as Inquiry	Teacher Autobiographies, Journals Critical Racial Incident Logs, and Text, Image, and Language Inventories and Interactive
Subject-Matter Content	ECRIE Literature Review /Research
Facilitators as Change Agents	Researcher Participant/Mentor

Understanding White Teacher Dispositions

In *White Women, Race Matters: The Social Construction of Whiteness* (1993), Frankenberg defines Whiteness in the following manner:

1. A location of structural advantage, race privilege;
2. A standpoint, a place from which White people view themselves, others, society;
3. A set of cultural practices that are usually unmarked and unnamed.

The racial privilege experienced by White society is the lens through which all interaction, interpretations, and decisions with the world are made. Within this definition we understand that the norm in society is Whiteness and therefore Whiteness has not been critically analyzed or deconstructed as we have done with other racial groups. This allows for the reproduction of White supremacy in the U.S., which is supported by Frankenberg's functions of Whiteness.

The first is the "essentialist mode" in which we accept that people of color are biologically inferior, less civilized, and less capable of performing to high academic standards. The second function of Whiteness is "color evasion," also known as color blindness. It represents the inability of Whites to see past their own race, making them believe that race is never an issue. Frankenberg's interviews of White women across the country demonstrate that White women want to disregard race as an issue in education. These women further believed that ignoring race separated them from essentialist racism, not acknowledging that they are in fact preserving the power structure needed to reproduce essentialist racism. The third and final function of Whiteness is "race cognizance" or "autonomy of culture." This allows for any racial inequities to be the product of capitalistic class structures rather than hegemony and socially constructed racism. In addition, Frankenberg found that "racist discourse frequently accords a hyper visibility to African Americans and a relative invisibility to Asian Americans and Native Americans; Latinos are also relatively less visible than African Americans in discursive terms" (p.12).This finding supports the matrix of domination discussed and presented by Patricia Hill Collins in *Black Feminist Thought*.

Race in Schools

In 1999, Julie Kailin conducted a qualitative study of 222 in-service teachers working in a medium-sized highly rated middle-class midwestern school district. She analyzed open-ended questionnaires for the perceptions White teachers have concerning race from open-ended questionnaires. The analysis can be categorized into three major themes: attribution of racial problems to Whites; attribution of racial problems to Blacks; attribution of racial problems to institutional/cultural factors. She found that the majority of White teachers navigated racism from what she terms "impaired consciousness." This translated into blaming the victim, tolerating racist White colleagues' behaviors through silence and nonconfrontation.

> One of the critical aspects of most White teachers' responses was how they framed their perceptions of racism, almost entirely positioning African Americans as the "other." In only 2 cases of nearly 200 were Latinos or Asians cited as targets of racism, and never as the cause. Blacks were the only group targeted as problematic. (p.744)

Kailin identifies the difficulty in changing teacher perceptions when she states, "Before people can be in a position to overthrow the racist paradigm, they must first be able to see how their own reality is socially constructed and how racism and White privilege have affected that construction" (p. 747).

Each individual has belief systems, ideologies that ground his or her perceptions. These ideologies also have conscious and unconscious components that allow participants to simply accept racial problems as belonging to an "Other" rather than making them critically self-reflect on the root of the issue or problem. In Frankenberg's study of White women, racism was rearticulated as economics and classism. Kailin's study demonstrated how Whites manifested racism through impaired consciousness, which blames the victim while ignoring their role as a perpetrator. In each case, Whites perceived that race was not, could not be, a defining factor in social inequities; therefore, Whites perceived racial problems in society as belonging to individuals, not groups. Kailin analyzed the difficulty of changing White teacher perceptions of race, unless they understood the reality of racism and White privilege in society. In other words, White teachers must change their ideologies concerning race from what Eduardo Bonilla-Silva terms color-blind ideology to what Bell calls a racial reality.

Focusing on the "individual" as in control of their destiny negates the structural aspects of racism in society. In *Racism without Racists*, Bonilla-Silva (2003,) explains how Whites perpetuate and justify a color-blind ideology. One central characteristic is the disconnect between what one says and what one does. Bonilla-Silva (2003) explains that

> Whites, despite their professed color-blindness, live in white neighborhoods, associate primarily with whites, befriend mostly whites, and choose whites as their mates. The contradiction between their professed life philosophy and their real practice is not perceived by whites as such because they do not interpret their hypersegregation and isolation from minorities (in particular blacks) as a racial outcome. (p. 179)

This disconnect is evident in Frankenberg's theory of "autonomy of culture" and Kailin's theory of impaired consciousness. In each case Whites worked toward disregarding race rather than confronting it.

Although the research on White teacher perceptions offers important insights into the mechanisms they use to perpetuate White supremacy, it does not investigate three important areas: (1) what racial ideologies are the participants entering the project with; (2) what are the concrete outcomes of the White teacher behaviors; and (3) what concrete material practices produce these outcomes? Research on teacher perception only reports on what the teachers "say" that can be a learned behavior in a society that professes to be egalitarian with equal opportunity for all.

Teacher Practice

Teacher-Student Interactions

In teacher-student interactions in integrated classrooms, Casteel (1998) asks, "Does race still influence the amount of acceptance and feedback that African American students receive from Caucasian American teachers in integrated classrooms?" (p. 1). The demographics of the participants are precisely stated. The 417 seventh-grade participants are broken down to their race, gender, and academic performance (p. 2). The instrument constructed, a teacher-treatment inventory observation system, was done so to precisely measure teacher behavior toward students in the classroom (p. 2). The instrument was a modified Brophy-Good Dyadic Interaction Observation System. Specific terminology in reference to the method used in the study was defined for clear understanding of the purpose and ensuing results (p. 2).

Two tables with mean values for the teacher-student interactions based on gender and race are discussed in detail in the results section of the study. A repeated ANOVA (Analysis of Variance) was undertaken for each of the sixteen observed variables leading to data that "reveals" the following results:

> African American students received more negative interactions from their Caucasian American teachers than the Caucasian American students; Caucasian American students received a greater portion of positive interactions such as being praised more often, receiving more positive feedback, and being given more clues by their teachers than African American students. (p. 4)

The researchers go on to discuss how these finding are consistent with previous studies and research, supporting and answering the stated purpose that "student interactions were racially biased in integrated classrooms, indicating that race is still a significant factor in the amount of contact a student receives" and that "there is enough data in this study to warrant petitioning school administrators and institutions of higher learning to instruct more effectively both pre-service teachers and current teachers in multicultural and racial awareness in the classroom" (p. 5).

The findings are consistent with the assessment of Ford (1985), Weinberg (1983), and Hillerman and Davenport (1978) that African American students are given less attention, ignored more, and praised less while Caucasian (White) students benefit from preferred treatment. In addition, it supports the work of Weinstein, Marshall, Brattesani, & Middlestadt (1982) and Good (1981) who have concluded that negative treatment from teachers negatively affects students' self-esteem. In all cases race was the primary factor and gender the secondary.

Teachers, Race, and Student Achievement

In 2001, Thomas Dee conducted a Quantitative Critical Statistical Analysis. He analyzed test scores from the Project STAR (for Student Teacher Achievement Ratio) databases, a Tennessee experiment begun in the 1980s in early childhood classrooms. Project STAR was designed to determine whether students learned more in smaller classes during their early elementary years. The experiment involved randomly assigning students to classes of different sizes. He found that students who had a teacher of their own race for at least one of the four years of the study tended on average to score 3 to 4 percentile points higher on standardized tests of reading and math than peers who had teachers of different races. In addition, this effect was cumulative for every year a student has a same-race teacher.

Dee recommends the aggressive recruitment of minority teachers based on evidence of biased behaviors of nonminority teachers. Prior work has called for recruitment based on the assumption that minority teachers are role models, making them better equipped to handle the issue of at-risk youth. Dee presents the first argument to recruit minority teachers based on empirical data with robust results. In addition, he presents the first data set that presents evidence of the cumulative effect of these gains. This exemplifies the importance of the social construction of academic identities and subsequently academic success.

In her article "The Road to Racial Equality," Beverly Tatum (2004) discusses critical issues surrounding identity and equity in educational settings. She calls for educators to work toward building communities and affirming identities of all students to support social and academic success in U.S. educational institutions. Tatum's work offers a space for educators to create common ground through identity affirmation:

> Affirming identity refers to the idea that students need to see themselves reflected in the environment around them—in the curriculum, in the faculty and staff, and in the faces of their classmates—to avoid feelings of invisibility or marginality that can undermine student success. Building community highlights the importance of creating a sense of belonging to a larger, shared campus community. The goals of affirming identity and building community are often perceived as being intension, but they are in fact complementary. Students who feel that their own needs for affirmation have been met are more willing and able to engage with others across lines of difference (p.34)

The implications of Tatum's recommendations become salient when we are willing to accept the work of critical education researchers such as Casteel and Dee in the area of student outcomes. In each case the power of the teacher to impact how students perceive themselves socially and academically is grounded in race. Casteel uses her study to move from the dominant discourse of multiculturalism that is color-blind (Frankenberg, 1993) to one that focuses on racial realism in education. Dee's study moves the recruitment of minority teachers from a discourse of role modeling based on student deficits in their social environments to a discourse of equity based on the racially biased behaviors of in-service White teachers. In each case the overprivileging of

White students is at the expense of the students of Color. Each of these studies and the collective work they have emerged from has focused on student outcomes. This body of research adds a new dimension to the work on teacher's racial perceptions discussed earlier in this section but still does not investigate (1) what racial ideologies teachers are entering schools with; (2) what concrete material practices produce these outcomes; and (3) how we can evaluate interventions.

Race Consciousness

Making Meaning of Whiteness
Alice McIntyre (1997) studied thirteen White undergraduate female student teachers. Each participant volunteered to take part in the semester-long participatory action research during the fall semester of 1992 in Connecticut. The group met for eight sessions and participated in semistructured interviews with McIntyre to make meaning of Whiteness and explore strategies to apply in teaching and research to "disrupt and eliminate the oppressive nature of Whiteness in education" (p. 7). McIntyre met with the group for two follow-up sessions the following semester. Three participants joined McIntyre and assisted with the data analysis.

The results suggest that for the participants, young White females in a private university, "white is normal, typical, and functions as a standard for what is right, what is good, and what is true" (p. 135). The students focused on the "Other" exhibiting a colorblind ideology, rather than reflecting on their role in a racist society. McIntyre used the term "white talk" to explain and label the coded language used by Whites to avoid critically self-reflecting on their own racialized worldviews. White talk, explains McIntyre, manifests itself as the uncritical acceptance of biased comments through avoidance, interruption, dismissing counterarguments, silences, and/or colluding with each other to create a "culture of niceness" that makes it very difficult to "read the white world" (p. 46).

Racial and Cultural Thinking
In 2000, Dr. Beverly Tatum and Dr. Phyllis Brown published the results of their two–year demonstration project entitled "Improving Interethnic Relations among Youth: A School-Based Project Involving Educators, Parents, and Youth." This project was funded by the Carnegie Corporation. It focused on the relationship between teachers, students, and parents in a small northeast school district with a 24% population of students of Color that was on the rise. The project comprised (1) an after school program for middle school stu-

dents focusing on identity; (2) parent outreach workshops; and (3) a professional development project for in-service teachers. For the purpose of this chapter I will focus on the teacher professional development component of this project.

In the first two years, eighty-three teachers participated. Of this group 83% were White, 62% were elementary teachers and the average years of experience were fourteen. Teachers examined their racial identities and attitudes and worked toward designing antiracist projects. They began the process of learning how to talk about race. The course, "Effective Antiracist Classroom Practices for All Students," "was designed to help educators recognize the personal, cultural, and institutional manifestations of racism and to proactively respond to racism in school settings. Topics included an examination of prejudice, racism, white privilege, and internalized oppression" (p. 2). Tatum reported that all participants heightened their awareness of the role race and racism play in the classroom and how each impacts student success in schools at different levels. In addition, after the grant funding ended, the local school district started funding the project, which is still in place as of this writing.

In 1995, Coleman and Deutsch reported that incidents of racial "intolerance and hostility" were increasing at all grade levels. This was and is compounded by the fact that the racial isolation that most Whites are raised in limits their understanding of People of Color (Zeichner, 1995). Underscoring the need for critical antiracist work to be undertaken with White teachers to promote equity in our schools, McIntyre, Tatum and Brown applied antiracist methods in their research. They organized their work around specific and concrete tasks. Teachers had to author a piece of antiracist work either in the form of a curriculum or action plan to implement outside of the professional development sessions. This method made it easier for teachers to dialogue about race. Since they could focus feelings of guilt or apprehension into their project, they felt productive in the dismantling of racism and White privilege.

In *Ideology, Discourse, and School Reform*, Zeus Leonardo identifies the problematic aspect to White teacher self-reflection concerning race and racism. He explains how action is an integral component to liberation:

> As privileged social subjects, whites who reflect on their own social status sometimes become inactive as if to divest one's powers means to become passive (Leonardo, 2003). White reflection does not rid oneself of white privilege. The trick is to use the privilege with which one is socially endowed, for political purposes in conjunction with the oppressed, against domination—not as leaders who colonize "the movement" but as partners in liberation. (p. 194)

To counter this tendency to become passive, we must move Whites toward antiracist models of professional development and conscious raising, as presented by Tatum and Brown. Their project gave its participants several roles to be partners in "liberation" as they learned about identity, race, student success while working collaboratively with peers and students. McIntyre, on the other hand, had a more difficult task, in that to simply reflect on one's position of power and privilege without a venue to apply a positive outcome can seem overwhelming and depressing to participants unprepared to discuss structural issues and how they can impact them. What separates antiracist work from critical antiracist work is a component of action. Action supports the transformation process for it gives hope that we can achieve an equalitarian educational community.

Summary

Research in teacher racial perspective, practices, and race consciousness shows that White teachers tend to focus on the "individual" as in control of their destiny, negating the structural aspects of racism in society, giving Whites the ability to perpetuate and justify a color-blind ideology (Bonilla-Silva, 2003). They code their language through "white talk" (McIntyre, 1997) and tolerate their racist settings through "impaired consciousness" (Kailin, 1999). One central characteristic is the disconnect between what one says and what one does. This disconnect is evident in Frankenberg's (1993) theory of "autonomy of culture" when issues of racial equity were essentialized and moved to a capitalism discourse. In each case Whites worked toward disregarding race rather than confronting it. In each case the power of the teacher to impact how students perceive themselves socially and academically is grounded in race. The one project that offered the greatest possibility of transformation from a color-blind ideology to a racial realism was that of Tatum and Brown. In addition, it offered an opportunity for action, affirming the teacher's identity as an antiracist. Action supports the transformation process for it gives hope that we can achieve an equalitarian educational community.

The question now is, where do White early childhood teachers place themselves when we talk about race? Research shows that White teachers typically place themselves in a color-blind ideology and discourse where Whiteness is normalized. This conveys the racialized dispositions of our early childhood teacher workforce, which are applied in classrooms through pedagogy.

Transformative Pedagogies

In the U.S., pedagogy has been predominantly interpreted and defined as teaching methodologies rather than philosophical or social theory. Donaldo Macedo (2000) explains that

> This seeming lack of distinction is conveniently adopted by those educators who believe that education is neutral as they engage in a social construction of not seeing. That is, they willfully refuse to understand that the very term "pedagogy" as my good friend and Colleague Panagiota Gounari explains it, has Greek roots, meaning "to lead a child." (From pais: child and ago: to lead) (p. 25)

Macedo wrote this passage in the 2000 introduction to Paulo Freire's *Pedagogy of the Oppressed*. His intention was to clarify to readers the use of the term by Freire in his writings. I agree with Freire and Macedo's interpretation of the term pedagogy and posit pedagogies as directed activities with the purpose of leading children to specific educational goals that are grounded in structural hegemonic ideologies or transformative ideologies. These ideologies are in turn supported by racial professional development projects presented in Chapter III.

As we have seen, assimilation was and still is a dominant pedagogy applied in early childhood that supports the new right. It is based in the mythology that children of Color have poor or low self-esteem[15] and are in danger of failing; therefore, assimilating to the dominate language and customs will boost the child's self-esteem and test scores. Sonia Nieto (2000) reviews research on assimilation and concludes, "Studies on student perspectives joins the expanding research that confirms the negative impact of assimilation on student's academic achievement." (p.290) Tolerance pedagogies are also prominent in our schools. In her book *Language, Culture and Teaching* (2002) Sonia Nieto identifies the inherent problems in the use of tolerance pedagogies:

> To be tolerant means to have the capacity to bear something, although at times it may be unpleasant. To tolerate differences means to endure them, although not necessarily to embrace them. We may learn to tolerate differences, but this level of acceptance can be shaky because what is tolerated today may be rejected tomorrow. Tolerance therefore represents the lowest level of multicultural education in the school setting. (pp. 339-340)

Tolerance insinuates that one is lesser than another and therefore must be put up with until you can find a way to disassociate with that individual. This context puts the dominant, in our case White students, at a distinct advantage. The major metaphor associated with tolerance is "We're all alike; we're all different," promoting in children an individualist worldview. There is no need to work out issues or concerns with the peer group or adults; you can simply tolerate their presence promoting a cultural pluralism ideology.

Culturally relevant pedagogy has been described by researchers and theorists as an effective means of meeting the academic and social needs of culturally diverse students (Gay, 2000; Howard, 2001; Ladson-Billings, 1994; Shade, Kelly, & Oberg, 1997). Gay (2000) asserts that culturally relevant pedagogy uses "the cultural knowledge, prior experiences, frames of reference, and performance styles of ethnically diverse students to make learning more relevant to and effective [for students]... It teaches to and through strengths of these students. It is culturally validating and affirming" (p. 29). Applied by Whites, the pedagogy of cultural relevancy can overessentialize the needs of racially segregated groups in its attention to academic achievement. Also a focus on academic achievement, based on standard measures of success, could become a new form of assimilation that allows teachers to co-opt and code the language of domination in a more culturally sensitive manner. This can occur due to racial biases White teachers are often unaware of having that may impede the application of culturally relevant pedagogies.

Racial biases in White teachers have been shown to have negative effects on student self-esteem, motivation, and academic performance. (Brophy, 1983; Cooper, Hinkle, & Good, 1980; Good, 1981; Meirier et al., 1989; Rabinow, & Cooper 1981; Robinson, Robinson, & Bickel, 1980; Weinstein, Marshall, Brattesani, & Middlestadt, (1982). These biases manifest themselves in the following ways:

1. Less attention and praise for students of Color (Casteel, 1998; Ford, 1985; Hillman & Davenport, 1978; Holliday, 1985; Marcus, Gross, & Seefeldt, 1991; Meire, Stewart, & England, 1989; Patchen, 1982; Washington, 1980; Weinberg, 1983);

2. Marked rise in reprimands of students of Color in multiracial classrooms (Aaron & Powell, 1982; Cecil, 1988; Hillerman & Davenport, 1978; Stevens, 1980; Troyna 1993);

3. When students respond correctly to a question, White students receive more praise (Aaron & Powell, 1982; Cecil, 1988; Ford, 1985; Hillman & Davenport, 1978; Holliday, 1985; Marcus, Gross, & Seefeldt, 1991; Meire et al., 1989; Patchen, 1982; Steven, 1980; Troyna, 1990).

These racial biases emerge from the perceptions we hold about groups of children we teach and interact with in our schools. Our perceptions that are grounded in our racial ideologies inform our pedagogies. Each of the predominant early childhood pedagogies discussed - assimilation, tolerance, and cultural relevancy - are therefore grounded in our racial ideologies, which emerged in teacher education programs and professional development projects. Racism has no middle ground; a community is either racist or not (Fanon, 1994); therefore, teacher pedagogies work toward either keeping the "status quo" in society or transforming educational setting to arenas of social justice and critical self-reflection. And just as racism has no middle ground, multiculturalism must not either. In an interview with Miner and Peterson of *Rethinking Schools Online* in 2001, Christine Sleeter explained why she stresses the importance of multicultural education as a struggle against White racism, rather than multiculturalism as a way to appreciate diversity.

> I keep going back to the fact that multicultural education came out of the civil rights movement. It wasn't just about "Let me get to know something about your food and I'll share some of my food." The primary issue was one of access to a quality education. If we're not dealing with questions of why access is continually important, and if we're not dealing with issues like why we have so much poverty amid so much wealth, we're not dealing with the core issues of multiculturalism. (electronic)

Antiracist Education

Programs in antibiased education, including antiracist education, have often focused on bringing diverse groups of individuals together to discuss concerns and improve intergroup relations. In the field of education, research has found that these programs rarely improve cross-cultural relations due to the fact that the material is too brief and/or superficial. We know that little or no effects occur on teacher behavior and/or attitudes simply by presenting facts and information about other cultures (Cotton, 1993). In addition, we know that "one-shot" or limited relationships between teachers and antibiased programs typically do not reduce bias or prejudice (Byrnes & Kiger, 1986-1987; Garcia, Powell, & Sanchez, 1990; Gimmestad & DeChiaria, 1982; Hart & Lumsden, 1989; Merrick, 1988; Pate, 1981, 1988). In fact these informational and one-shot antiracist projects have been shown to increase intolerance (Zeichner & Hoeft, 1996). Change in race relations can occur only when Whites acknowledge and accept that racism is a White problem and begin the process of eradicating it.

To counter these norms we must identify the ways in which we make our racial ideologies visible and then critique them "to uncover the vested interest at work, which may be occurring consciously or subliminally, revealing to participants how they may be acting to perpetuate a system which keeps them either empowered or disempowered" (Geuss, 1981 as quoted in Cohen, 2000, p.30). In classrooms we do so through the language we apply, the texts we choose, and the images we display. It is through these artifacts that knowledge is produced and identities are informed, impacting current standard measures of success. "Race is a critical and defining feature of lived experiences that young and old and people of all colors reflect upon, embody, challenge, and negotiate" (Fine et al., 1997), informing our group identities. And race "works to inform one's relationship to knowledge and its production" (Ladson-Billings, 2001, p. 266). Therefore, the relationship between student measures of success, student identity formation, and teacher racial ideologies made visible through their pedagogies are of great importance to the future of our young children.

If we value an egalitarian society we must understand the permanence of race and racism, of what Derrick Bell terms a racial reality (1992), which I have presented through statistics on the achievement gap—White early childhood teacher dispositions and racial identity construction/deconstruction. I present that the need for transformative pedagogies focused on antiracism as an imminent critique of the racial reality in U.S. schools. And that antiracist transformative pedagogies (1) acknowledge relative positions of power, authority, and privilege; (2) accept the need to be accountable for; and (3) take action against the structural racism in our society.

The ability to transgress White supremacist structures in society is embedded within what bell hooks (p. 15, 1994) calls engaged pedagogy that "emphasizes well being...meaning that teachers must be actively committed to a process of self-actualization that promotes their own wellbeing if they are to teach in a manner that empowers students."[16] Her work in engaged pedagogy is informed by Freire's concepts of conscientização and liberatory learning and Nhat Hanh's concepts of the teacher as a healer, viewing a union of "mind, body and spirit"[17] as the goal of education. hooks contends that a teacher must first heal herself or himself to attain the freedom needed to enter engaged pedagogy with their students.

The process of self-actualization presented by bell hooks (1994) gives us the ability to embrace change through the recognition that the knowledge produced in universities and informing our practices is based in "biases that uphold and maintain White supremacy, imperialism, sexism, and racism (and) have distorted education so that it is no longer about the practice of freedom."[18] Establishing this truth on the production of knowledge allows us and our students to practice freedom through transformative pedagogies.

In order for White teachers to support positive and equitable racial identity construction, they must first understand their position of power within our racialized system of schooling. White teachers must take an active role in antiracism if they are to ensure each child possesses the ability to form positive and equitable racial identities, working toward breaking the social cycles that sustain racism. Many, if not most, teacher education programs include modules in multicultural education (Grant & Secada, 1990; Ladson-Billings, 1995). What is not common is the application of an intentional and informed antiracist framework (Cochran-Smith, 1995; Kailin, 1994) and theory. If teachers are passive in their antiracism attempts, they may actually perpetuate racism and the patterns of behavior that are actively racist. Henry Giroux (1997) identified what he believes to be the major problem associated with a White teacher self-identifying as antiracist; that is, the terms "White" and "antiracist" seem mutually exclusive. To eliminate this dissonance, Giroux (1992) believes teachers need to become "border crossers." First, they must accept their race, gender, sex, and class, and second, they must not try to eliminate their ability to be antiracist, but justify the need. Building on Henry Giroux's theory of border crossing, Christine Sleeter's call for critical multiculturalism and bell hooks' theory of engaged pedagogies (1994), I present antiracist transformative pedagogy in three levels of development for White teachers: acceptance, accountability, and action.

- *Acceptance* of racial realism. We all have racial identities and this has a direct relationship on how White children and children of Color construct and deconstruct racial identities.
- *Accountability* for our group identity, White racial hegemony. Individual identification as White is not synonymous with White group identity; therefore, we must be accountable for the racial reality our system of schooling imposes through the overprivileging of Whites and disprivileging of students of Color
- *Action* grounded in racial realism works toward an egalitarian educational environment as it counters White racial hegemony. Acceptance without commitment to change perpetuates White racial hegemony.

Classroom pedagogies are the outcomes of racial professional development projects in the U.S., and as such do not promote transformative antiracism. Once we accept that they in fact have racial ideologies and understand their need to be accountable for how they impact our students, we are ready to take action. We can communicate with our students and families and enter into antiracist projects within our educational communities crossing borders toward RET if we do not lapse into guilt. Guilt impedes action by encouraging a false sense of inadequacy thus eliminating one's need to effect a change. In addition, it brings further attention to the White teacher (rather than the students of Color) through sympathy from peers, leading us to a need to understand the relationships that exist between White identity development and antiracism.

White Identity and Antiracism

Since racists are White, understanding models of White identity development is necessary to interrupt cycles of racism. In her model of White racial identity development, Helms (1990, 1993) describes six identity statuses (formerly called stages) that characterize a White individual's pattern of responding to racial situations in the environment:

1. *Contact*: begins as one encounters Black people either physically or metaphysically. This individual has a superficial and inconsistent awareness of Whiteness.
2. *Disintegration*: begins when one is conscious of (although conflicted) and acknowledges their Whiteness.
3. *Reintegration*: is marked by the conscious acknowledgment of a White identity. Whites are idealized and Blacks are denigrated.
4. *Pseudo-independence*: is the first phase in redefining a positive White identity. It is a phase of intellectualizing and acceptance of one's own race as well as other races.
5. *Immersion/Emersion*: is the honest appraisal of racism and the significance of Whiteness, in other words learning how to become antiracist. It is often marked by strong emotions.
6. *Autonomy*: is an ongoing process where Whites are open to new information and new ways of thinking about race and culture.

These statuses are situational, and more than one status may be used in any given context, meaning that this model is not a topography—classifying racist behavior of Whites into discrete categories—as outlined by many White identity models in Table 9, but rather a matrix each of us navigate daily. Helms' model has been empirically tested and is widely accepted in the field of White racial identity development. In addition, its use of statuses allows us to analyze White behavior in specific contexts and explore the relationships between emotion and action in multiple situations that can lead to an internalized multicultural identity. Helms terms this identity as a nonracist White in the autonomy status. For Helms (1993) this represents the healthy component of Whiteness that all Whites should strive for, a place of harmony within one's emotions, attitudes, and behaviors.

Table 9: White Racial Identity Development Topologies

Re-searcher(s)	Kovel (1970); Jones (1972) Gaertner (1976)	Terry (1977)	Ganter (1977)	Hardiman (1979)	Carney and Kahn (1984)
Topologies	Dominative Racist	Color-blind	Protest and Denial of Racism	Acceptance	Stereotyp-ing
	Aversive Dominative Racist	White Blacks	Guilt and Despair	Resistance	Detached Intellectuals
	Aversive Liberal Racist	New Whites	Acceptance and Action	Redefinition	Denial or Anger
	Nonracist			Internaliza-tion	Reform White Identity
Key Language	Blacks, Racism	White, Racism,	Whites Racism	Whiteness, Racism,	Ethnicity, Culture,
	White Superiority	Black Pluralism		Nonracist	Pluralism

White women often become excited by Helms' model since it offers hope for disassociating oneself from the term racist, by entering into autonomy and taking on a nonracist identity. In their desire to be viewed as someone who accepts and understands how race works in society, they often co-opt the language without reflecting on observable outcomes or changes in their own behaviors, focusing on their personal perspectives. Since historically U.S. antiracist professional development has focused on personal narratives, race consciousness, and teacher perceptions without documenting observable changes or outcomes, this should not surprise us. RET offers us a theoretical framework to change this phenomena in antiracist professional development.

Antiracist Professional Development

Most projects that directly address race in educational settings fall under antiracist professional development. I distinguish between research-based professional development studies and teaching resources that include seminal work in the field of Whiteness studies, such as McIntosh's identification and naming of specific examples of White privilege presented in *White Privilege: Unpacking the Invisible Knapsack* (1988). Although both are related and important, the need to document changes in teacher strategies and perspectives demands data to support that antiracist professional development has the ability to transform teacher ideology. For these reasons, I use the following criteria in antiracist professional development research projects; they all have been directed toward in-service classroom teachers, identify antiracism as the focus of the professional development (not one of a matrix of isms), are implemented over an extended period of time, typically a semester, and identify racists as White. In addition, I have organized them under these accepted subcategories of racism:

- *Individual racism* manifests itself in individual attitudes, beliefs, values and behaviors.
- *Cultural racism* manifests itself in the cultural rules, values and standards that disadvantage people because of their race, color or ethnicity.
- *Institutional racism* manifests itself in the practices, customs, rules and standards of organizations. (Jones, 1981)

Individual Impact

In *Teaching/Learning Anti-racism* (1997), Derman-Sparks and Phillips share ten years of teaching a course to move graduate and undergraduate students from proracism to antiracism. They view this process as a developmental approach. It consists of four distinct phases carried out over a semester course:

1. Beginning explorations of racism;
2. Exposing the contradictions;
3. Transformation to an understanding of self and society;
4. Antiracism as a new beginning;

This developmental approach, applied over a semester, is well documented and has shown the most changes in self-reported individual teacher racial beliefs (Kailin, 1999, Ladson-Billings, 2000, 2001), perceptions, and race consciousness (McIntyre, 1997; Tatum & Brown, 2000; Zeichner, 1996).

Cultural and Institutional Impact

The study conducted by Lawrence and Tatum, *Teachers in Transition: The Impact of Antiracist Professional Development on Classroom Practice*, has documented teacher-reported cultural and institutional racism changes in public school settings. Tatum explains, "The course was specifically designed to help educators recognize the personal, cultural, and institutional manifestations of racism and to become more proactive in response to racism within their school settings" (Lawrence & Tatum, 1997a, p. 163). The study reported that "changes in classroom practice" is limited by its reporting method. Forty-eight teachers self-reported one hundred and forty-two antiracist actions, classifying them into three categories: (1) the quality of interpersonal interactions among school and community members; (2) the curriculum; (3) the institution's policies regarding support services for students of color (p. 167). In addition, participants reported that maintaining antiracist work without support was difficult at best.

Each of these studies emphasizes the need for alternative models while offering important insights into how we can extend antiracist professional development toward RET. I present the next step as transformative antiracist professional development grounded in critical action research to move equity agendas forward. ECRIE is one such project. It was informed and designed based on this need and offers practical tools to document tangible outcomes of professional development toward closing the achievement gap in early childhood.

Critical Action Research as Professional Development

The case for inquiry insists that reflection must be tied to larger social processes and promote acts that commit, if not contribute, to transforming them. It also acknowledges that the reality that changes begin with local places such as schools, and with individual people like teachers. (Leonardo, 2003, p. 235)

I modeled ECRIE on the work of Kemmis and McTaggart (1988, 1992) who advocate that "Action research is concerned equally with changing individuals, on the one hand, and on the other, the culture of the groups, institutions and societies to which they belong" (1992, p. 16). In ECRIE, critical action research is a systematic form of ideological self-reflective inquiry by participants, with the specific intention of increasing their understanding of how they manifest their hegemonic ideologies in their classrooms. This understanding will then assist classroom teachers as they apply antiracist pedagogies, which in turn allows for the changing of individuals, groups, and institutions. Our role as a participant researcher in critical action research necessitates that we not only apply antiracist professional development strategies but also challenge dominant racial ideologies that do not promote social justice.

Weis and Fine discuss in *Speed Bumps* (2000) how we as researchers can "come clean at the hyphen" or reveal our position:

> It is now acknowledged that we critical ethnographers have a responsibility to talk about our identities, why we interrogate what we do, what we choose not to report, how we frame our data, on whom we shed our scholarly gaze, who is protected and not protected as we do our work. (p. 59)

Understanding the sensitive nature of a participant researcher in action research demands we closely follow principles such as those presented by Kemmis and McTaggart (1981, 1988, 1992) in their ethical principles for the guidance of action research (see Appendix B) and Strike's (1990) ethical principles of evaluation (see Appendix C). In addition, we must strive to be reflexive (Hall, 1996) in our analysis, applying the same rigor to ourselves that we apply to others through authentic data, democratic relations, and antiracist self-reflection in our role as a participant researcher. We must remember that no one method has the ability to communicate truth. Therefore, ECRIE is not only grounded in action research but also draws on semiotics, historiography, and hermeneutic methods in an effort to investigate the complexity of racial ideologies and the work of antiracist professional development. Semiotics holds that all artifacts are modes of communication in a given culture similar to verbal language. It consistently looks for interrelationships between institutional structures and individual consciousness through the exploration of artifacts. This process works toward exposing manifestations of power, how they are reproduced, and how consciousness is constructed (Britzman, 1991; Hodge & Kress, 1988; Manning & Cullum-Swan, 1994; Scholes, 1982). It is within semiotics that our research team can begin uncovering manifestations of our racial ideologies through artifact inventories of the images, texts, and language we apply in our classrooms.

Equally important is understanding our place in history and how the power and privilege of Whites has evolved at the expense—socially, psychologically, and economically— of all People of Color. Historiography offers us the hope of social justice. Kincheloe (2003) contends that "To change, to educate themselves and/or the world, humans must connect past injustice to present suffering; they must fathom the mind-set of their ancestors in order to expose the forces that have created present conditions" (p. 243).

Where semiotics and historiography focus on artifacts and social outcomes—tangible manifestations of ideology—hermeneutics offers us an interpretive dimension to investigate the relationships between the concrete and abstract, parts and the whole. It is here that we can begin to explore meaning through thick description, reflection, and dialogue with colleagues, in an effort to "tie interpretation to the interplay of larger social forces (the general) to the everyday lives of individuals (the particular)" (p. 247).

RET in New Mexico

ECRIE is one method grounded in critical action research of addressing the need for teachers to understand the reality of racial ideologies, how racial ideologies impact student racial identities, and how we can create racially equitable classroom environments. It builds on the work of antiracism, Whiteness, and early childhood scholars with the intention of moving antiracist professional development research past perception documentation to observable changes in teaching strategies. Classroom text, image and language artifact inventories, focused classroom observations, and racial incident logs create the framework from which the inquiry group examines and interprets the racial ideologies they made visible in their classroom. Change strategies potentially can create tools that White teachers can use to combat institutional racism. But they cannot be documented or implemented until teachers accept, understand, and identify the racial ideologies they make visible in their classrooms daily. Identification of ideology moves teacher reflection from a passive act to one that can transform through the application of antiracist change strategies. ECRIE consists of the following components grounded in antiracist transformative pedagogy:

Racial Ideology
- Acceptance: we all have racial ideologies.
- Accountability: identification of the ideologies we make visible in our classrooms through artifact inventories and teacher texts.
- Action: Teacher designed

Racial Identity
- Acceptance and understanding of the impact racial ideologies have on early childhood racial identity construction/deconstruction.
- Accountability: Identification of the racial identities we privilege in our classrooms through artifact inventories.
- Action: Teacher designed

Racial Equity
- Acceptance and understanding of the impact antiracist strategies have on promoting racial identity equity.
- Accountability: Identification of strategies we can apply to create antiracist learning communities that promote racial identity equity.
- Action: Teacher designed

This process assists White teachers and teachers of Color as they identify strategies for transforming their racial ideologies and classroom pedagogies to reflect antiracist ideals and practices toward RET.

I conducted two ECRIE courses in New Mexico. The first course consisted of five White teachers over one semester and the second of eight mixed-race teachers. I distributed 2400 flyers to secure these thirteen participants. They all worked at schools identified as in need of improvement, with one-third to one-half of their students coming from multilingual families. In addition, they had small populations of White monolingual students. They counseled me on what they thought would be a respectful data collection schedule, focusing on teacher artifacts and ideological critique grounded in critical race theory. We worked out a schedule of readings and a flexible timeline. Their insights and excitement about the project inspired and guided our work. Next I asked our group what would make discussing and challenging dominant views of race more accessible to larger numbers of teachers. What emerged was this:

- The need to align research and professional development to state mandates, specifically licensure requirements;
- The desire of teachers to do research;
- Teachers guide the work, not administrators;
- Administrative support and respect.

On the basis of these recommendations, I applied to the Professional Development Council (PDC) at UNM and had a course on racial identity development approved as a sanctioned professional development course for teachers in New Mexico. In addition, I aligned the course to state licensure requirement, offered it free of charge and offered a graduate credit option. Although I distributed the 2400 flyers, teachers in schools later informed me that they never received information. My greatest obstacle in New Mexico was getting across information to teachers since I could not directly distribute the flyers. All materials were approved for distribution first by individual districts and then by school principals.

Challenges

ECRIE was conducted over thirteen weeks and began with two groups of teachers. Text and image artifacts collection began with thirteen teachers in eight classrooms; teachers kept critical racial incident logs, participated in inquiry groups, and read selected texts on how racial identities inform classroom communities. Of those thirteen teachers, eight completed the project and the section "Lessons from the Field" will reflect their four classrooms.

Our group consisted of seven preschool teachers and one kindergarten teacher. Of these eight, two self-identified as White, Irish; two as Mexican; and four as Hispanic (see Table 10). All were women and six were monolingual. I did the first data collection, while the rest of the data were collected and shared by the teacher researchers. This allowed for a balance between the delivery of new knowledge, discussion and content, and reflection on individual and group data sets. Filmed sessions of ECRIE in teacher classrooms were not permitted in New Mexico and five teachers discontinued their work due to gatekeeping, teacher overload, and the sensitive nature of race as I will now discuss.

Table 10: ECRIE Participant Information

Number	Race	L1/L2*	Grade Taught
1	Mexican	English/Spanish	Preschool
1	Mexican	English	Preschool
4	Hispanic	English	Preschool
1	White	English	Preschool
1	White	English/Spanish	Kindergarten

* L1-first language, L2-second language

Gatekeeping

I worked with three urban school districts in New Mexico and each posed a form of gatekeeping that impeded the ability of the teachers of ECRIE to fully complete the projects they began. District 1 allowed me to distribute my flyers but would not allow me to directly communicate with individual schools to follow-up on the distribution. I had to wait to be contacted by individual administrators. This method of advertisement limited my interactions with real people, making it quite easy for the schools to ignore the project. It also did not allow me to elaborate on the integrity of the work or the potential it held to impact test scores for students while empowering teachers. I had, however, managed to contact individual teachers who expressed interest, but without administrative support they were concerned that their work would be viewed as unnecessary and impact their annual reviews.

District 2 had allowed me to offer ECRIE as a professional development course the year before I wanted to document the process through action research. I was quite excited since many of their teachers helped inform and design the original project. I communicated to their central office that I had been approved through the University of New Mexico's Internal Review Board (IRB) and would send in my application to conduct research on ECRIE in these schools. District 2 had adopted a new review process and my application went before their board. This was a closed process and the applying researcher was not allowed to attend or defend the application. Gaining approval through my IRB was a lengthy process because the topic in discussion was race but I knew the attention and ethics demanded by them was an indicator of quality and rigor. My teachers were organized; they had begun the readings; they were keeping critical racial incident logs and participating in discourse inquiry groups. What we could not do was enter classrooms and film for our "Racial Discourse Observation Protocol."

Typically the review process was quick and the rigor of the IRB process respected. When I did not hear from the district 2 office, I called and left messages over three weeks. When I finally received my application package back, I was told that it was not approved because of noninterest by the district and that they felt it lacked practical relevancy and technical adequacy. I was directed to stop implementing ECRIE and turn over to the district office any collected data. No feedback was offered other than "You are welcome to resubmit at any time in case research priorities change," clearly telling me that my denial was because of the topic of race. Teachers were interested enough to participate in the design and now the research application. In addition they believed that understanding how to support equitable racial identities in school was relevant and practical in order to address the achievement gap, defining race as a topic of great importance. Unfortunately these views held by teachers did not have any effect on the district's decision. I tried to call and discuss the matter with the office of research, but none of my calls was answered.

In New Mexico, protocols in the IRB process allow district level administrators to discontinue research, regardless of teacher or principal support. Action research is grounded in teacher identification of critical educational needs, which they in turn reflect and self-reflect on deeply as they collect and analyze classroom data through theoretical lenses. If a district has the control to stop this process, then action research loses any ability to transform and empower teachers, students, and educational communities. In addition, since district 2 had teachers already organized and dedicated to ECRIE and a racialized achievement gap, how could a school district ethically or morally state that they were not interested?

District 3 offered the most hope for success. Six White teachers were identified by the district office and principals approached for participation. They represented both new and experienced teachers and each wanted to move past talking about equity and be part of a movement to take action. The level of enthusiasm was high, but as we began planning, it became clear that we were expected to keep a low profile so as not to bring attention to our work, which would impede our ability to complete the project. This dynamic led to a loss of enthusiasm by the participating teachers. We entered into ECRIE honest and clear that we were interested in action research as a form of student and teacher empowerment. Each of us felt as if we had to hide our work; we began to monitor our interactions with other teachers and administrators in the district. We agreed that although the district had some allies, who believed in action research and the need to look at alternative ways to address the racialized nature of the achievement gap, they were not ready to accept ECRIE as an empowerment model of professional development.

Teacher Overload

Teachers felt overwhelmed by NCLB mandates and testing. I worked with many teachers in the New Mexico public schools who inquired if I would continue offering ECRIE as a professional development course. These teachers were interested in participating but requested that I offer it between term exams that lasted three to six weeks at the beginning of the school year and three to six weeks at the end.

I was impressed that at a time when teachers are being deskilled through the adoption of scripted curriculum materials, these teachers would have the time and energy to support ECRIE and challenge the district's decisions. But I was also concerned that the stress of this added work would impact their personal and professional lives in the form of sanctions, leading to teacher burnout. This was specifically why in district 3 we chose to discontinue ECRIE. Teacher overload also guided how ECRIE was finally implemented in New Mexico. We worked outside the schools and collected data that was teacher generated, to keep our autonomy.

The Sensitive Nature of Race

The overwhelming majority of teachers and administrators in early childhood are White and the fact that they have power and privilege over People of Color was uncomfortable for them. I worked in three large urban school districts in New Mexico. In the majority of the schools administrators did not distribute professional development flyers I provided. When I discussed this with administrators familiar with my work, I was told that principals and instructional coaches are directed to not waste professional development time on projects that are not aligned with direct instruction and absolute outcomes that can be assessed empirically. They were encouraged to screen projects for their teachers and distribute only what they felt would support greater testing outcomes for the students.

When I realized that after six years of planning and working in New Mexico I would not be able to complete or report the filmed component of my data collection in public school classrooms, I questioned my role in this project. At first I became consumed with what I viewed as failure. But finally I realized that ECRIE would only be as powerful as the access it is allowed and I learned from our action research groups that we were breaking new ground. I also recognized that if I could present a theoretical framework, RET, to ground this work within, not only my project but also those of future early childhood educators could fight for their procedures and research methodologies to gain greater access in the future. Each of these teachers renewed and inspired me to work through my interpretation of failure and follow-through with our project. And so we did.

ECRIE: Lessons Learned from the Field

All teachers who completed ECRIE in New Mexico said they would continue it if it was offered again; they thought that the process encouraged growth, and they appreciated having a community of fellow educators to discuss sensitive issues with such as race. They also believed that without a sustaining community as we had created, it would be hard to continue what they have started. The mixed-race group of teachers felt that a change in power dynamics occurred midway through the course due to the content of the material we covered. White teachers began to listen and wait for teachers of Color to comment first. Teachers of Color began to offer counternarratives to White hegemonic ideology on a more frequent and regular basis. In addition, teachers observed more proracial messaging across White students and students of Color. We identified specific components of ECRIE that led to these outcomes. This was the power of artifacts, common language and racial incident logs.

In-Group Messaging: *The Power of Inventorying Artifacts*

Although all teachers self-identified themselves as aware of the importance of race in education and committed to social justice text and image inventories, in all classrooms books and images privileged Whites. From the data we collected on in-group messaging and racial identity consistency, we found that White students in these classrooms were receiving more positive in-group messaging on a daily basis than the students of Color.

The majority of the teachers were shocked when the first text and image inventory identified on average that 69.8% of the artifacts privileged White English-speaking males; 27.6% White English-speaking females; and a little over 1.5% male and females of Color, with less than 2% of that subgroup being in a language other than English. They all came into the project self-identifying as teachers dedicated to social justice and had difficulty accepting that they had not seen this trend in the images and artifacts in their classrooms. As we moved on through the project, discussions, text and images brought to our attention the need to have an organizational method in place to periodically self-reflect on to ensure we did not fall into old patterns. Only two of the eight teachers were not surprised and both of them had communicated on a content-knowledge test that children do in fact make sense of their world through race. The other six teachers were surprised and communicated on their pretest that racial awareness, prejudice, and racial identities do not impact children or develop until the elementary school years, a perspective that changed after their participation in ECRIE.

One technique that the teachers applied was to make sure that any book displays that a child interacted with consisted of literature that balanced racial images with positive racial in-group messages. Next they reviewed the literature and images to ensure that gender and language balances associated with positive in-group messages were also present, since the data also showed that it was not only White but also White English-speaking males who received the most positive in-group messages. Another technique applied by a group of three teachers was trimesters. They were concerned that their lack of knowledge on how to choose the texts and time would inhibit their ability to always balance the positive in-group messages in their texts, so they created a log and made sure that over a three-month period they balanced the positive racial messaging communicated through their texts and images. It was critical to this process that I communicate the individual nature of one's progress. We researched authors for authenticity to their subject matter and when in doubt of a racial, cultural, linguistic, or ethnic perspective sought advice from parents, coworkers, and scholars of that group.

Each of the preschool teachers attended a two-day conference in New Mexico and three attended a session on Native American children's literature. During the ECRIE inquiry group that followed, they discussed how they felt empowered as they sat and began critiquing the books for the session for racial, cultural, linguistic and ethnic authenticity before the presenter began her presentation. They identified this as a critical incident in their professional identity and that it gave them great confidence to now share that information with others. When I asked why, they said they now had the language, methods to assess books, and the research. In addition, being able to share their work with other teachers at the conference made them feel competent. One teacher commented, "sometimes you stay out [of] conversations because you just don't understand what they are talking about, be we knew and we could share experiences we have had looking for authentic authors."

A Shared Language: *The Power of Discourse Inquiry*

We based our inquiry discussions on Van Ausdale and Feagin's book *The First R: How Children Learn Race and Racism*. Prior to each session I handed out a glossary of key terms that would be in our readings, and we played with them. We went over pronunciation, guessed at meanings, and then connected them to our own practice. For teachers who came from varied educational backgrounds ranging from certificate programs to graduate school, it was an exercise in community building. In evaluations of the course every teacher identified that playing with words and language prior to having a discussion relaxed and entertained them. Several teachers said that they now were playing with words in their classrooms before reading a book and have begun bringing in more sophisticated literature because their children loved learning new and unusual words by engaging in this wordplay. As a researcher I applied this strategy to assist with equalizing each teacher's ability to discuss theory and research. But as I found out this became a point of empowerment.

Jean was a self-identified Hispanic female teaching assistant with extensive experience—over sixteen years. She was quiet and did not offer her opinions in the first three sessions. During one meeting in which we were discussing pedagogy, methods, and ideology, she commented, "If I knew that all these highbrow words were simply textbook terms for what I do every day, I may have gone back to college!" Jean's comments began a chain reaction of interchanges within our group on how unintelligent and cautious much of the language of NCLB has made them feel. Regardless of the degree held by any one in our group, Jean's honest assessment of the jargon used in education brought a unity among us that transformed the conversations each week. In addition, it gave her voice in a forum she historically found threatening.

Jean became the first teacher to discuss Whiteness from her lived experiences. She commented, "most of the people in charge of us are White, and most of the people that tell us what to do are White, yet most of your children, are not White. I wonder if they know what our kids need!" I witnessed the reaction of Amy, our White kindergarten teacher, and Trish, our White preschool teacher. Both were looking down, unsure of what to comment. The Hispanic and Mexican teachers' eyes grew wide and they sat. Finally Amy, who is in a biracial, bilingual marriage, looked up and said, "yeah, that's what we do" and the entire group broke into laughter, relieved that she and Trish did not get upset, cry, or challenge the comment. Amy's clear, honest assessment of the reality of our educational system was the second transforming incident during our talks. Katy, a Mexican teacher, commented that she typically was uncomfortable having such discussions with mixed-race teachers since she was usually taken as a disgruntled worker, or Whites would become overcome with guilt, drawing all attention to their issues, not hers.

Bringing teachers together around a table on a common topic that is historically sensitive gave each of them the courage to be honest because they were there for the kids, each dedicated to issues of social justice and equity. All of us agreed that if the White teachers had become full of guilt and found the need to cry and ask for absolution, the dynamics would not have been as productive in our inquiry group.

Perception versus Reality: *The Power of Critical Racial Incident Logs*

All the teachers expressed that the two definitive events that made them realize they were blind to the reality of race in their classrooms and creating a version of race based on their perceptions. These events were the artifact inventories, ensuing statistics, and keeping the critical racial incident log. Six of the eight teachers did not believe much of theory presented in *First R: How Children Learn Race and Racism* until they themselves documented racial incidents in their classrooms. These were definitive moments that shifted their system of beliefs from the perception that they were practicing RET and made them identify the ways to begin the process of applying the tenets of RET. Each vignette revolves around physical characteristics of the children. Prior to documenting these critical racial incidents teachers in our group often challenged a child's ability to make sense of their relationships based on race, feeling that they were not capable of seeing or applying racialized social norms.

Seeing Whiteness—Racial Authenticity

Getting Pretty

Trish, a White preschool teacher, discussed how three young girls would meet each morning and critique each others' hair styles—the straighter the better—and noses—the smaller the better. Trish found one student, LaRhonda, pulling and tugging at her shoulder-length curls. When she asked LaRhonda what she was doing, LaRhonda looked up into Trish's eyes with great seriousness and replied, "Getting pretty! you know..." But Trish did not understand what LaRhonda was hinting at and decided to share this incident with her colleagues and me. Our group decided that we would apply a strategy to support positive in-group messaging to LaRhonda, the reading of racially authentic literature. Trish was cool to the idea but wanted to make an effort to support LaRhonda. She decided to read poems by Eloise Greenfield from her book *Honey I Love*. The children laughed and giggled as Trish read the poems and soon they began to discuss what they loved. On one particular morning LaRhonda shouted, "I l-oooo-ve the pictures!" Trish was a bit surprised because she felt the illustrations were secondary to the poems. She asked LaRhonda why she loved the pictures, and she received the following response: "Because they look like me, look at her hair and look at her nose, it is just like mine." The two girls who would meet with LaRhonda each morning to critique hair and noses turned to LaRhonda and said, "Ooooooh, I wish I looked like Eloise Greenfield too." LaRhonda smiled wide and long, and Trish said she just about glowed.

It was at this moment that Trish, a White teacher, realized that their notions were steeped in race. Her students were creating norms of what was pretty, based on racial features in the classroom, privileging White and light-skinned children. The reaction of her students amazed her. Over the course of a year she added to her racially authentic literature and said she could never teach any other way again. She explained that her students became more intrigued by diversity and less with conformity. And that she became comfortable discussing diversity not only from gender and language perspectives but also racial perspectives.

For Amy, a White teacher, the power of White hegemony became visible during her efforts to eliminate racial conflict from her room through the use of animals.

The Pink Bow

Amy was aware that race was an important social construct in her class. She used photographs and pictures of children, along with animals, to alleviate racial tensions that could arise when one group is overrepresented. What she did not anticipate was the prevasiveness of race in her classroom even with these interventions. She had a bear chart that showed emotions and feelings. She found it soothing and useful when having discussions with her students, until she happened to observe an interaction between two girls in her class. Sally was White and Terry African American. They were both admiring the bear chart and chatting about their work in the room. Sally got very excited and pointed to a bear in the top left-hand corner, "look," she said to Terry. Terry turned and tried to see what she was pointing at, "the pink bow," she added to Terry. "I should have known," said Sally. "What?" replied Terry. "It's White! Of course the White bear has the pink bow, everybody knows White bears are the prettiest and best, brown bears are dull and dirty looking."

Amy was stunned and was in disbelief when she witnessed this event. For Amy this led to a deeper understanding of the structural aspects of White racial hegemony, a painful and needed realization. We cannot erase race from our classrooms but must face it with calm resolve and focused interventions. She took the bear chart down and replaced it with pictures of her students and made sure that Terry had her choice of the feeling she wanted associated with her photo in the new display.

Seeing Shades of Race—Racial Balance

You're Too Dark

Monique had an incident between a Black boy, Ronald, and two Hispanic girls, on the playground. The girls told Ronald, "You're too dark so we don't like you!" Ronald came inside crying and told Monique what had happened. Monique shared that he was crushed and that he would play with every child in the school. Monique immediately interupted this event by bringing all the children to a group meeting. "I had the children put one arm out and we looked at them all and talked about all the different colors and shades we were. After that "LONG" conversation they (the Hispanic girls) never teased him anymore—but still they would not play with him."

He No Look Like Me

Monique also shared an incident that took place between a young Hispanic boy, Michael, and a White girl, Sarah. "One of our boys liked to play with the girls. He wanted to play chase with Sarah and she became upset and came to me. "Michael, he bother[s] me!" I talked to Sarah and Michael. Michael said, "I want Sarah to be my friend," and Sarah said to me, "he [is] not look like me so I don't want to play with him." Monique thought this could be based on gender since she had seen Sarah's mom telling her that girls should play with girls and boys with boys. Sarah had witnessed such biased conversations and had good success interpreting this cycle, encouraging cross gender play. Monique discussed how lucky they were to have so many friends at school. She explained that among the friends some are boys and some are girls. However, when Monique discussed that girls and boys can be friends, Sarah replied, "NO, not boy, he don't LOOK like me, so I don't play with him!"

These events were difficult for Monique, a Hispanic teacher, to accept since she could not immediately address them and did not want children that she identified with to suffer or cause suffering to other children. She shared, "it is more difficult when it is your own people." As she discussed these events within our group she realized that not every situation had an easy answer and that she would work on balancing the positive cross-racial messages that children were exposed to during their school days. She immediately assessed that her books and classroom images were sterile and hegemonic. Now that race was visible and tangible, she not only accepted the racial reality playing out in her room, she also made herself accountable to changing those dynamics within her school community. She knew she needed to observe, listen, and continue to take actions until a change occurred.

Her first step was to use authentic images of her children and balance them by race and gender in her class. Her critical racial incidents explained how important not only race was but also shades of race. She said that after using authentic images, more positive cross-racial conversations about each child began to happen spontaneously in the classroom, especially when she displayed an image of cross-racial and cross-gendered play. Although Ronald did not play with the two girls who said he was too dark, other friends sought him out more often after the class meeting and Sarah did in fact begin playing with Michael. Monique just needed to not stop intervening.

Seeing Race within Race–Positive Racial In-Group Messaging

You're Not Dark Enough

Shelly began, "we have one child in our classroom who is Black, Tambra. Recently another child who is Black, Aliesha, joined our class. Tambra became very upset, crying all the time. When the teachers asked her what was wrong, she would reply that she missed her mom. It was getting to where we could not stop her from crying. Eventually this child did not want to come to school. The teachers then informed her mother and grandmother. Neither could explain why Tambra was so sad. Then one morning the grandmother came in and said she knew why the child was so sad. She explained that Aliesha had told her she wasn't Black enough, because she was a lighter shade than her."

This incident made Shelly, a Mexican teacher, realize the presence of racial prejudice even within the same race. At first she did not know how to approach this incident. If Whiteness and racism were hard to discuss, this seemed even harder. The group offered a solution grounded in in-group messaging. We had been focusing on authentic literature and images and balancing them by race and gender, but we now knew it was time to go deeper and make sure that within each race we had diverse representations that explained the reality of this socially constructed identifier in our society. Shelly decided that the best way would be to ask Tambra's family for suggestions and then ask the school librarians for assistance. She found that most of the books were in fact of light-skinned Black and African American children. This led to a discussion around Aliesha's in-group messaging. Shelly could find some pieces of literature that Tambra identified with, but it was more difficult to find for Aliesha. The group suggested she apply Monique's techniques of direct intervention and using students' photos, encouraging cross-racial and now within-race collaborations to capture and print for classroom displays. Shelly was not ready to have intervention meetings but found the use of photography empowering. As with Monique, it allowed for informal discussions between Shelly and her students around their relationships as she worked toward promoting positive racial in-group messaging within group as well as cross-racially.

ECRIE Interrupted

When we ended ECRIE, it seemed incomplete, unfinished, interrupted. We remained connected for a while and then resumed our normal lives and I wondered how much of our learning would survive. Or as the teachers already discussed, would it be too hard to continue to have such discussions without a support group? Although each of us witnessed great changes in how our students self-identified and then interacted in classrooms, would this sustain them or like us do they need a support group? Would we continue to apply racial balancing, positive racial in-group messaging, and authentic counterhegemonic texts? This will depend on if and when early childhood educators accept the realities of race in the lives of our young, hopeful, and powerful children and their equally hopeful and powerful families.

RET in South Carolina

I remember the moment I told my family that I had accepted a faculty position at the University of South Carolina. They gasped because they remembered the state of being I was in when I was stationed at Fort Jackson in the early 1980s. Friends and family both asked, how I could study race in South Carolina. While stationed at Fort Jackson, I experienced severe racial isolation and segregation while visiting the city of Columbia as an advanced individual trainee. The outcome of which was the inability of White trainees and trainees of Color to socialize off the Fort Jackson base. As I walked through Columbia, I witnessed, People of Color move aside as Whites shared sidewalks, enter different stores and socialize in different locations. Racism was overt in South Carolina at this time, but for all the racial, linguistic, and cultural diversity in many states, there still lacks recognition of the covert racism that was and currently is a part of the lives of children. In South Carolina, and more precisely in Columbia, recognition of the role of race and racial ideology is surfacing. The confederate flag was an unchallenged source of pride in the 1980s where as today it is a source of debate and open embarrassment not only by People of Color but White allies. Relocated in 2000 from the State Capitol Dome, to the Statehouse grounds with a confederate Soldier Monument, the flag draws national and local criticism. The initial leadership of the NAACP began this project, which continues today. Senator Joe Biden said before the NAACP rally in March of 2007 that

> If I were a state Legislator, I'd vote for it to move off the grounds _ out of the state.... As people become more and more aware of what it means to African-american here, this is only a matter of time (Washington Post January 15, 2007).

And in April of 2007 USC head football coach Steve Spurrier openly stated as he accepted a leadership award from the City Year Columbia, an affiliate of the Americorp group that,

> I realize I'm not supposed to get in the political arena as a football coach, but if anybody were ever to ask me about that damn Conferderate flag, I would say we need to get rid of it. I've been told not to talk about that. But if anyone were ever to ask me about it, I certainly wish we could get rid of it (April 16, 2007 Associate Press).

Increasingly, respected public figures both locally and nationally are taking on issues of racial equity in South Carolina.

Established as a slave colony, South Carolina has an intimate relationship, ownership of, and responsibility for race and racism. In addition, a deep sense of southern independence has allowed principal and teacher autonomy to survive in educational communities and not be absorbed by central offices as has happened in other parts of the country. One mediating factor may be the University of South Carolina's history in the Professional Development School (PDS) Network. As a professor, I teach onsite at local public schools with real children, real teachers, and real administrators. I have regular meetings and conversations with my PDS schools and healthy exchanges of ideas. And my colleagues have worked with and through individual schools, charter proposals, and entire districts in an effort to affect systemic change. Although not a solution in itself, PDS partnerships offer opportunities to bridge higher education and public schools. For scholars dedicated to transformative action research, school based teaching and teacher empowerment, this network is a productive model to conduct one's work within.

The relationships I built within this model not only supports preservice and graduate students, but also allow me to align my research agenda to the goals of the schools in true collaborations. For critical Whiteness scholars such as myself, this is a needed bridge to cross for access and acceptance in public education. I have spent several years getting to know schools and their communities and have identified teachers in PDS schools, that participated in a RET project embedded in a joint preservice/in-service action research collaborative. The project was piloted as a component of a required preservice teachers course on building communities of learners. Participating teachers participated in an ECRIE study group. As in-service teachers apply new RET teaching strategies, they document their sessions for our preservice teachers to discuss and use as they become comfortable in applying similar strategies to support race, gender, sex, class, linguistic, and ability identities. The course culminates in a meeting where the preservice teachers present identity-based curriculum analyses and the strategies they would apply in classrooms to support equitable and productive learning communities, while the in-service teachers present their data on the relationships between teacher ideologies, in-group messaging and student outcomes. Embedding RET projects in required courses and using real data to drive the discussions are one way to shift current hegemonic norms in society. This has the potential to then create a new official knowledge in early childhood education that empowers a child to self identify, rather than being labeled with socially constructed racial identities that are embedded in notions of White privilege.

Undergraduates and RET

When presenting RET work and projects to undergraduates, we have additional barriers than when working with in-service teachers who have experiences to draw upon in classrooms. I have observed specific behaviors that students use to deal with the stress of self-reflecting on ideological beliefs that instructors must navigate. Typically, the first is intimidation. After presenting qualitative and quantitative data on how children make sense of their racial ideologies, students have ask if I am a real professor or working toward being one. I politely answer, "real." The next behavior is challenging authority. They have asked, "who grades my work, you or the Early Childhood Department?" Again I calmly answered, 'I do" The final response is often silence, a nonparticipatory objection to the material. The irony is that the minute we began discussing gender, each woman in my class turns into a staunch advocate of any and all strategies I present. Therefore, each of these barriers became my strategies. Prior to presenting and discussing RET; I discuss gender, language, and sexed identities, building their critical lenses. Then I present details on my own research addressing the "real professor" concern and follow up with a discussion on academic freedom, integrity, professionalism and education equity as tools of social justice. This sets a smoother stage for discussion around race and racism.

Whiteness Studies

Critical texts on Whiteness such as *You Can't Teach What You Don't Know* and *White Teacher* are powerful in undergraduate programs but need structures built in to allow for the emotions they will elicit. I have students write a formatted one-page reflection that is due two days before class. I review each one and then make decisions on the debriefing session based on these documents. This serves several purposes, first I know who is having the most difficult time with the material, second, it is a place for the students to focus their opinions and thoughts as they work through their emotions, and third, it gives the instructor a space to self-reflect on how to most effectively support the students. In addition, each week we read text and narrate critical racial incidents students observe in their field placements. Juxtaposing their book reflections on the lived experiences of children they observe assists in decentering their attention from the "I" to the "we." I have observed ideological trends from the I to the we while studying archived collections of critical incident and reading reflections, where students first react, reflect, and then respond, often discussing how the text has made them see children in a more critical way.

Margie entered my class reserved, attentive and strong. Her confidence did not come from arguing, but from reflecting deeply. Where many students verbally reacted to their reading reflections, Margie preferred to share her thoughts on paper and reflect on my responses and questions prior to entering into class discussions and become a leader and role model for her cohort. Her first response to *You Can't Teach What You Don't Know* began,

> These readings physically make me ill! I am guilty of turning my head when it comes to facing the realities of the history of my own race [White]. It is easier to me not to think about race and culture on a daily basis. I feel horrible about everything white people have done in the past. (Margie, January 29, 2007)

After spending time observing classroom interactions and documenting them in her critical incident log she shifted her focus from herself, the "I" to society or the "we." She stated, "We ought to seek this understanding [of race] not because we stand accused of the sins and excuses of our ancestors, but because we are committed to equitable opportunities and outcomes for our students." (Margie, February 12, 2007)

Janice began the term actively participating in class discussions. While reading *You Can't Teach What You Don't Know*, she immediately engaged in the text,

> As I read I agreed with many things, however, if he [Howard] were speaking to me I would probably be just like the others. I would not want someone telling me I was a bad person. I felt like there was another way to handle it, but as I continued to read I realized that maybe there isn't. People become too comfortable in their lives. (Janice, January 29, 2007)

But as the term progressed she began to disengage from classroom conversations. She was engaged in ideological dissonance. Her shift from the "I" to the "we" occurred when she made a direct and unnerving connection between the text and her own life. Janice wrote the following in her journal response,

> The part where he [Howard] talks the dean driving a BMW through a white neighborhood was interesting to me. We do not think about it often, but it is true. People see a black person driving a nice car they automatically assume the worst. I have heard people say before "he is a drug dealer" just because he was black and driving a nice SUV. "I am definitely starting to see Howard from a different perspective. At first I felt like he was the one pointing fingers and placing blame. I see that it goes much deeper, he wants us to become aware of the social problem [racism] and try, as teachers, to make a difference. (Janice, February 12, 2007)

After this incident, Janice once again joined in classroom discussions and ended her journaling on the book with the following entry, "We simply have to open our minds up and see things from a different perspective. That is how we find change" She gained confidence and insights into her role as a future educator dedicated to equity.

Paley's *White Teacher* evokes strong initial emotions based on the title. Whites typically do not acknowledge they have a race. Student journals reflected discomfort and shame from the term White, which they viewed as a synonym for racism as evident in their journal entries. Twelve of twenty responses in once class reflected the following sentiments.

> When I first saw the text *White Teacher* on my list of books to read for this course I was very apprehensive about reading it; in fact I was almost appalled that the title was on the list at all, not to mention how uncomfortable I was buying it. (Ashley, March 24, 2008)

> At the beginning of the year, when I went to buy the book *White Teacher*, I was a little nervous about purchasing the book. When I checked out, the cashier gave me a very funny look and asked me where I found the book in the store. The title of the book made me feel uneasy about reading the book. I had no idea what Vivian Paley was going to discuss within the pages. (Kate, March 24, 2008)

Grounded in the day-to-day activities of a kindergarten classroom, Paley's book offered unique opportunities for early childhood students to move past their initial fears on race and racial identity. Once students such as Kate and Ashley passed their initial discomfort they began to accept the reality of race in their lives and profession as reflected in subsequent journal responses,

> I had connections to this book all throughout. The things discussed can be easily found in any school, playground, and class all over America. In my particular class-

room the class is about half white students and half black students. It is absolutely amazing to see how this is entirely the case in every way shape and form. When on the playground they immediately split into these groups, when called to the rug they do the same, in the cafeteria they split themselves there too. Although this is a very obvious and reoccurring practice found in my particular classroom it is never addressed. (Ashley, April 12, 2008)

This book was a surprisingly great and interesting read. Vivian Paley is a wonderful writer. She describes situations in such a clear and honest light. I love that she doesn't dance around when it comes to the subject of race. I feel as if I was reading her thoughts, kind of like reading her journal. Most books are so busy trying to be politically correct that I just want to throw the book across the room and call "bull". How are we ever supposed to overcome any sort of racial divide if we are always tip-toeing around the subject. (Kate, April 12, 2008)

Kate, Ashley, Janice and Margie's journeys are not atypical when time is dedicated to making clear and consistent connections between RET research, theory and the lived experiences of our children as well as ourselves. As more new teachers begin this journey of self-reflection and discovery they become the future for closing the achievement gap.

Some students will blame such texts for causing them stress, using unfair language and being mean to Whites, but I explain that for People of Color this is a stress they do not have the privilege of not facing on a daily basis. Therefore, it is fair and equitable that if we want to teach diverse children we must spend time first listening to and teaching ourselves about how People of Color view our educational system and our methods of instruction. I challenge them to use these insights to reach out and begin the process of connecting with diverse families and establishing meaningful and honest relationships that promote pride for all races, to include Whites.

Embodiment

During ideological shifts some White students will begin to embody emotions associated with seeing their own race apply racism. We can assist them through this process by sharing similar situations that each of us experienced, thus becoming role models of empowerment, rather than leaving them hopeless. I remember precisely the moment I became aware of overt racism in my school and community as a classroom teacher. It was in 1997 in CT.

Faces

I dreamed. I dreamed of faces. I dreamed of faces of great sorrow, sorrow born of murder, destruction, and indifference and I dreamed of pain. Pain so deep, so insidious that I would wake in the night cold with sweat, my heart pounding. One night I caught my breath and sketched. Once I started, I could not stop. I sketched on receipts, napkins, cereal boxes at home, breakfast trays, and recycle papers in my classroom. Finally I copied them on to canvas, using leftover paint from the classes I taught and I hung them on walls and studied them. What were those pictures? What did they mean? Why would they not leave my subconscious? A week after I painted those faces, my kindergarteners and I were getting ready to visit one of our parents at work. The project grew out of conversations on how and what my students thought they should learn about in school. One student said, "each other." This brief statement led to weeks of talks and the group thought visiting parents at work was good because "parents can't leave their jobs to meet everyone in the school."

Lashonda's mother, Venita, walked through the door. She tossed her head back, laughed, and brought herself down to the level of the children. "Well who is exciTED TOday!" Smiles, laughs, and giggles filled the room. Venita had a way of making every child feel special. Charles and Tanya were cuddled in her lap reading a book while we waited for the morning meeting. Tammy, the first-grade teacher, walked to the doorway from her room next door to see if any students were staying at school. I told her "no." She was about to leave when she looked at Venita, smirked at me, and whispered, "OH nooo. Don't tell me she's going..." Tammy's eyes widened, her neck extended, and her shoulders tilted back. She looked at me as if I understood what she thought, which I didn't. "Yes, why" I asked. "You'll see." Is all Tammy offered before leaving.

As I turned to enter the room I saw Venita—Charles and Tanya were still in her lap—but she had her head cocked to the right, eyes cast downward, large, dark, her neck pulled in, her shoulders slouched. I was frozen, I knew this face, I had painted this face, I had felt this face.

Venita saw me; I smiled and walked to her, "Time to get them moving Venita," I joked. "Was she talking about Me?" she asked. "Yes, wanted to know if you were coming with us." I replied. "Bet she had a mouthful to say about me." "Not really, she was just concerned that you were going on the trip. I didn't get it," I said. Venita looked at me, "You CONcerned?" "Nope, should I be?" I replied. Venita laughed, tossed her head back, and scooped up Charles and Tanya,"You are MINE!" and the three of them went off giggling.

It was on this morning with Venita and my kindergarteners that I understood my dreams. They were the embodiment of the perceptions that the predominantly White teachers and administrators in my school imposed upon and used to justify differential treatment of parents from the east side of the park I lived on, those who lived in the projects, those who were not White. Over the following year I had many experiences similar to this one I am sharing with you now. They not only happened in school, but also in the local stores and playgrounds. These were my neighbors, my friends, my parents, my students.

It was the first time I can remember in my life when the concept of group identity became a visceral experience for me. I of course cannot truly understand the oppression any of these people suffer since I am White and live with great confidence born of privilege and the position associated with that power, but I dreamed and embodied emotions that have never left me. These emotions have pushed me toward exploring ways to communicate it with other White teachers and to reflect on the structures in society globally, nationally, and locally that persist in creating barriers for all of us as we work toward applying agency in situations such as Venita and I experienced. I was always disappointed that I didn't directly address Tammy at that particular moment, but I myself was just beginning to understand how these systems of oppression were embedded in our daily routines, through texts, images, and language we each applied. How we made our ideologies visible.

Sharing moments such as these as a White instructor can humanize the process of embodiment, build trust, and make clear to your students that you authentically understand the stress you are asking them to face. Following this up with current empowerment projects you are engaged in and with other teachers will give them a place to aspire to, rather than leaving them only with guilt, which, as I discussed, takes attention away from the needed change. A focus on proactive change can keep the group moving forward. The greatest compliment an undergraduate student gave me during these sessions was, "Dr. Earick, you really like talking about race," and I replied, "yes, and I hope someday you do too."

Making Visible What Once Was Invisible

Just as White students work through ideological shifts, so do students of Color, and we must be ready to support their emotions as well. At the beginning of our course, we typically discuss our racial, ethnic, cultural, and linguistic heritages in class. Most students enjoy this and find many commonalities with their peers that they did not know existed. It builds community. But not all will share their heritages for a variety of reasons. For some it is the fear of political prejudice in a post 9-11 society, for others it is an issue of mixed heritages and family distress and still for others it is a self-imposed invisibility internalized by our interpretations of U.S. history.

After completing an ECRIE module on Indigenous Peoples in our integrated curriculum course, seven of my twenty-four students shared that they were Native American. They said that they did not practice the ways of their grandparents or extended family members and therefore had not seen themselves as true Native Americans. When I asked why they did not talk about their heritage when we discussed our ancestry, their responses were, "I didn't think it mattered," "I never think about Native American as a race or ethnicity." After discussions around the relationships between identity, academic achievement, and racism, their views changed on what it meant for them to be Native American. There was an acknowledgment that by making this part of their lives invisible, they did not need to critically analyze how Indigenous Peoples were treated as a group. Each of my students found a new component to their work, making their race visible and promoting equitable presentations of their lives. This is especially salient since the majority of Indigenous Peoples in South Carolina, as well as nationally, do not have federal recognition, which emphasizes their invisibility. One technique that supports valuing racial identities is data-supported role-playing.

Are You In My Network?

The use of data in role-plays has the potential to transform thinking towards RET. It offers an opportunity to make visible the tangible outcomes of in-group messaging on children and encourages empathy through the embodiment of cross-racial emotions. This activity is most powerful when presented in a large lecture hall with seventy-five or more participants. Prior to the exercise:

1. Prepare a short presentation on early childhood racial identity formation from chapter IV.
2. Set up your room: Place four chairs in your space that allows for all participants to view the chairs. You will need four volunteers, one White female, one female of Color, one White male, and one male of Color. Due to the emotional impact this could have on your volunteers of Color, place their chairs in the middle. In this way they will have each other as support once the reality of this event unfolds.

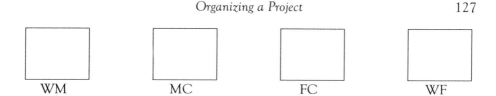

WM	MC	FC	WF

3. Read *Are You in My Network?* Vignette

We are going to explore and make visible the tangible outcomes of in-group messaging in real classrooms and then discuss what this means to children in our classrooms. Amy is an early childhood kindergarten teacher in New Mexico who speaks dual languages and self identifies as a Social Justice Educator. She is comfortable not only discussing gendered, sexed and linguistic identities but also race. She is a dedicated professional who participated in a RET project in 2005 and 2006 to self reflect on her teaching pedagogies in an effort to support her racially diverse learners. As part of ECRIE (Early Childhood Racial Identity Equity), participants inventoried over 360 artifacts both print and images and coded them by race and gender as to the recipient of positive in-group messages in her classroom. It was found that 69.8% of her texts privileged White Males, 29.6% White Females and .75% males of color and 1% females of Color and less then 2% non-speakers of English. For this activity we will focus on speakers of English. I will round the numbers and we will build networks of positive in-group messages for four students, one White female, one White male, one female of Color, and one male of Color through third grade, since this is when identity consistence occurs. Could I have four volunteers, one from each identity group?

4. Present the Data

I will read to you how many positive in-group messages each student will receive over the course of four years. For each message one classmate will join our student volunteers.

Race/Gender Identity	In-group text/image messages K-3rd Grade	In-group teacher messages K-3rd Grade
White Female	3 X 4 = 12	4
Female of Color	1 X 4 = 4	1
White Male	7 X 4 = 28	0
Male of Color	1 X 4 = 4	0

The groups of students, who join in the exercise, create networks of positive in-group messages around our volunteers showing who is over privileged and who is underprivileged in educational settings. This visual representation becomes the platform to debrief the data.

5. Debrief the results in relationship to the research on early childhood iden-
    tity equity and academic achievement. Consistently, students as well as
    colleagues, who have observed the exercise, tell me this changed how they
    viewed the impact of in-group messaging on academic success. It's power
    lies in truth. Amy's data is directly related to national achievement scores.
    As the volunteer representing the male of Color always realizes, he has a
    very high probability of being placed in a special education classroom
    while his White classmates excel. White males consistently outperform
    White females and females of Color know they will have less educational
    opportunities then their White counterparts as shown in standardized
    tests, advanced placement courses, graduation rates and future wages. Fo-
    cusing the students on supporting their interpretations of the implications
    of this exercise based on known outcomes in education keeps them from
    shifting the discussion to their feelings of guilt or shame. This is one way
    to use embodiment as a tool to validate the need to identify strategies to
    balance racial in-group messaging in our schools.

Next Steps

> To interrupt the cycle of racism, young people need to understand how prejudice and
> racism operate in our society. They also need to feel empowered to do something to
> change it. However, many educators are unskilled at talking about racial issues. Many
> teachers have had limited opportunity to explore these issues in their own education,
> and they hesitate to lead discussions about racial tensions for fear that they will gen-
> erate classroom conflict. (Lawrence & Tatum, 1997a)

Each of these teachers and students gives every early child teacher and
educator a gift, the gift of hope that each of us can and must engage in social
justice through the application of transformative pedagogies grounded in RET
if we want to close the achievement gap. The racial reality of our public education system demands decades of reform, but the thirteen teachers of ECRIE
have already begun that process. They empowered me to design and implement RET projects with preservice and in-service teachers who allow for action
research to develop and thrive in public education. Now we need a collective
effort by others in our field.

We know that White supremacy has a long history dating back to the fifteenth and sixteenth centuries when Whites explored, colonized, and exter-
minated peoples in the name of progress and entitlement (Balibar &
Wallerstein, 1991; Mills, 1997; Spring, 1998). We also know that White supremacy is currently working in U.S. society through a "new racism" (Bonilla-
Silva, 2005, pp. 17-18) that it is increasingly invisible and covert, avoids racial
terminology, and is a rearticulation of past racial practices characterized by Jim

Crow. We only need to look at the racial nature of the achievement gap to see each of these elements of the new racism. Historically, a class-based argument has been used to justify the achievement gap; yet we know that the highest number of children living in poverty is White (NCCP, 2006; U.S. Bureau of the Census, 2004). Whites represent 39% of all children living in poverty, Latinos represent 31%, Blacks 23%, Asians 3%, and all other peoples represent 4% (NCCP, 2006); yet Whites consistently outperform children of Color on standard measures of success in public education, take advanced courses, and gain economic and cultural capital as the predominant racial group graduating from universities and colleges with advanced degrees. These facts call for higher education, public school districts, and political policymakers to no longer ignore or perpetuate the invisibility of racial dynamics in student outcomes or covertly promote racism through a color-blind class-based argument. We must critically analyze professional development and provide opportunities for teachers and educators to accept the reality of race, accountability for their actions, and gain the needed tools to take action toward RETs. Each Department of Education, each public school district, and each policymaker is our future and the future of our children. I leave you with this thought:

Reality....
See it
Live it
Change it

With Respect and Resources Toward
Empowerment

RDOP
(Earick, 2005)

RDOP- Racial Discourse Observation Protocol
Version: Teacher Self-reflection (TSR)

TO BE USED IN CONJUNCTION WITH AN ECRIE ACTION RESEARCH STUDY GROUP

I. Background Information

School_____ Date of Observation _____

Teacher Reflecting: _____

Scheduled length of Class_____

Length of observation_____

Grade Level(s) Taught: Pre-K K 1 2 3

Number of Years Teaching _____

Gender: M   F

Racial Heritage:_____

School District: _____

Certification: _____

II. Class Demographics

A. What is the total number of students in the Class at the time of the observation?

O 15 or fewer	O 26–30	O 61 or more
O 16–20	O 31–40	
O 21–25	O 41–60	

Is the diversity of this Class characteristic of the composition of the school as a whole?

Racial Diversity

O Yes	O No	O Don't Know
Give a count when possible.		

Gender Diversity

O Yes	O No
Give a count when possible.	

III. Class Context

Rate the adequacy of the physical environment for facilitating racially equitable student learning.

1= Met   2= In-Progress   3= Beginning

	1	2	3
1. Class resources: (Texts in classroom balance racial and gendered images and privilege position)	O	O	O
Rational/Justification: (Give % of each gendered and racial group).			
2. Room arrangement: (Students have opportunities to work in mixed gendered and mixed race groups for academic and social events).	O	O	O
Rational/Justification			

IV. Class Description and Purpose

Please fill in the instructional strategies observed student race/gender, DSD, and CDF used in each five-minute portion of this Lesson in the Matrix Chart. There may be one or more strategies and frames used in each category during each interval.

A. Instructional Strategies

P	Presentation/lecture	PM	problem modeling
PWD	presentation with discussion	RSW	reading seat work (if in groups, add SGD)
CD	Class discussion	D	demonstration
HOA	hands-on activity/materials	CL	Co-op learning (roles)
SGD	small group discussion	TIS	teacher/instructor interacting with student
AD	administrative tasks	LC	learning center/station
UT	utilizing digital educational media and/or technology	OOC	out-of-Class experience
A	assessment	I	interruption
WW	writing work (if in groups, add SGD)	SP	student presentation
Other			

B. Student Race/Gender (as self identified by your families or students- add categories as appropriate). Samples listed below

AA	Asian American	LAT	Latino/Latina
AFA	African American	Wh	White
Bk	Black		
IP	Island Pacific		
IPA	Indigenous Peoples of the Americas		
HIS	Hispanic	ND	Non-disclosed

C. Curriculum Discourse Phase (CDP)

After reading, *Interactive Phases of Curricular and Personal Re-vision with Regard to Race* (McIntosh, 1990), code your CDP status.

P1	All-White History
P2	Exceptional Minority Individuals
P3	Minority Issues, minority groups as problems, Anomalies, Absences, or Victims
P4	The lives and cultures of people of color everywhere as history
P5	History redefined and reconstructed to include us all

D. Teacher/Student Discrete Skills of Discourse (DSD)

After reading, *The development of conversational and discourse skills*, (Pan & Snow, 1999), code your DSD

Code	Discourse Building	
1	Describe	Giving account of attributes
2	Extend	Increasing an account of attributes
3	Question	Posing doubt or uncertainty for clarification
5	Challenging	Demand an explanation, justification, or proof
6	Relate	Significant connection to one's lived experience
O	Open Question	Multiple answers are appropriate and encouraged
C	Closed Question	One answer is expected
D	Directive	
U	Ultimatum	

E. Context

AK	Academic Knowledge	Focus on content
SK	Social Knowledge	Focus on community building

F. Privilege

SP	Student Perspective	Student discourse is validated
TP	Teacher Perspective	Student knowledge is corrected or ignored

Matrix Chart

Time in minutes:

	0-5	5-10	10-15	15-20	20-25	25-30	30-35	35-40	40-45	45-50
Instruction Type										
Student(s) Race										
CDF										
DDF										
Context										
Privilege										

A. Using your Matrix Chart, reflect on the following questions:

What students did you give the most positive in-group messages to?

What students did you give the most negative in-group messages to?

What students did you not give any in-group messages to?

Whose knowledge was privileged more, the students or the teachers?

B. In a few sentences, describe the lesson you reflected upon and its purpose. Include where this lesson fits in your overall unit of study, syllabus, or instructional cycle. Justify your statement with data from each section of this observation protocol.

Teacher Questions

PRE-CLASS

What will you be doing in the lesson today?

How much do you know about this topic?

How comfortable are you with this topic? Why?

What instructional strategies do you think you will apply in this class to address racial equity in your classroom?

POST-CLASS

How did you accomplish in your lesson today?

Did you learn new information or do you want to extend your knowledge on this topic?

What instructional strategies did you apply in this Lesson to address racial equity in your classroom?

After reflecting on this data, are their instructional strategies you would like support in extending or changing? If so please give specific goals.

Ethical Principles for the Guidance of Action Research[1]
(Kemmis & McTaggart, 1981)

Observe Protocol	Take care to ensure that the relevant persons, committees, and authorities have been consulted, informed, and that the necessary permission and approval have been obtained.
Involve Participants	Encourage others who have a stake in the improvement you envisage to shape and form the work.
Negotiate with Those Affected	Not everyone will want to be directly involved; your work should take account of the responsibilities and wishes of others.
Report Progress	Keep the work visible and remain open to suggestions so that unforeseen and unseen ramifications can be taken account of; colleagues must have the opportunity to lodge a protest to you.
Obtain Explicit Authorizations	This applies where you wish to observe your professional colleagues; and where you wish to examine documentation.
Negotiate Descriptions of People's Work	Always allow those described to challenge your accounts on the grounds of fairness, relevance, and accuracy.
Negotiate Accounts of Others' Points of View	Always allow those involved in interviews, meetings, and written exchanges to require amendments that enhance fairness, relevance, and accuracy.
Obtain Explicit Authorization Before Using Quotes	Verbatim transcripts, attributed observations, excerpts of audio and video recordings, judgments, conclusions, or recommendations in reports (written or to meetings).

Negotiate Reports for Various Levels of Release	Remember that different audiences require different kinds of reports; what is appropriate for an informal verbal report to a faculty meeting may not be appropriate for a staff meeting, a report to [a] council, a journal article, a newspaper, a newsletter to parents; be conservative if you cannot control distribution.
Retain the Right to Report Your Work	Provided that those involved are satisfied with the fairness, accuracy, and relevance of accounts that pertain to them, and that the accounts do not unnecessarily expose or embarrass those involved, then accounts should not be subject to veto or be sheltered by prohibitions of confidentiality.
Make Principles of Procedures Binding and Known	All of the people involved in your action research project must agree to the principles before the work begins; others must be aware of their rights in the process.
	Accept Responsibility for Maintaining Confidentiality

Ethical Principles of Evaluation[1]
(Strike, 1990)

Due Process	Evaluation procedures must ensure that judgments are reasonable; that known and accepted standards are consistently applied from case to case, that there are systematic and reasonable procedures for collecting and testing evidence.
Privacy	This involves a right to control information about oneself, and protects people from unwarranted interference in their affairs. In evaluation, it requires that procedures are not overtly intrusive and that such evaluation pertains only to those aspects of a teacher's activity that are job related. It also protects the confidentiality of evaluation information.
Equality	In the context of evaluation, this can best be understood as a prohibition against making decisions on irrelevant grounds, such as race, religion, gender, ethnicity, or sexual orientation (without placing them in a socio cultural context or placing them as the explicit purpose of the research).
Public Perspicuity	This principle requires openness to the public concerning evaluative procedures, their purposes, and their results.
Humaneness	This principle requires that consideration is shown to the feelings and sensitivities of those in evaluative contexts.
Client Benefit	This principle requires that evaluative decisions are made in a way that respects the interests of students, parents, and the public, in preference to those of educational institutions and their staff. This extends to treating participants as subjects rather than as "research fodder."
Academic Freedom	This requires that an atmosphere of intellectual openness is maintained in the classroom for both teachers and students. Evaluation should not be conducted in a way that chills the environment.
Respect for Autonomy	Teachers are entitled to reasonable discretion in, and to exercise reasonable judgment about, their work. Evaluations should not be conducted so as to unreasonably restrict discretion and judgment.

Preface

1. Hispanic is used by the U.S. Census Bureau as an inclusive term for any one who speaks Spanish or claims to be of Spanish descent. If one was from Spain this would be accurate, but since speakers of Spanish are from a large number of countries, this explanation is incorrect. Speakers of Spanish languages and descent include, but are not limited to, Latino, Mexican, North American, Mexican-American, Hispano, and Chicano. For further discussion, see the Hispanic Research Institute at the University of New Mexico, http://www.unm.edu/~shri/1/1about_shri.html. For the purposes of this book I will use the terms applied by the statistical reporting agencies.
2. Historically, Black has been used by the U.S. Census Bureau as an inclusive term for people of African descent. Since Africa is not the only country of origin of individuals who self-identify as having a racial heritage of Black and not all peoples from Africa claim Black as a racial heritage, this description is incorrect. The term African American, which has gained political and popular support as an alternative label, is in debate. Many believe it should be a term associated with those Black Americans who were kidnapped and enslaved, distinguishing them from those who freely entered the country, while others believe it should be used regardless of nationalism. For the purposes of this book I will use the terms applied by the statistical reporting agencies.
3. As present in Dr. Allen's Whiteness Seminar at the University of New Mexico.

Chapter 2

1. For an extensive critique of the role of beneficiaries and subordinates in society, see Mills (1997, p. 63)
2. Orfield, G. (1995). *Schools more separate; Janet Ward Schofield.* "Review of Research on School Desegregation's Impact on Elementary and Secondary School Students." In J. Banks & C. Banks (Eds.), *Handbook of research on multicultural education* (pp. 597-617). New York: Simon & Schuster; and Orfield, G., & Eaton, S. (eds.) (1996). *Dismantling desegregation: The quiet reversal of Brown v. Board of Education.* New York: New Press.
3. Taken from the NAEP (National Assessment of Educational Progress) Web data tool (http://nces.ed.gov/nationsreportcard/naepdata/search.asp), U.S. Department of Education, NCES, NAEP, selected years 1992-2003 Reading Assessments.
4. The science assessment was reported only for fourth grade. For more detailed information on the achievement gap in New Mexico, see the NCES' report card at http://nces.ed.gov/nationsreportcard/states/profile.asp.
5. The 2003 Albuquerque Partnership "New Mexico Achievement Gap" report focused on the need for highly qualified teachers and for University of New Mexico to enroll non-White students. In addition, the report stated that "the year 2004 differs from years past in terms of quality and equity questions about education in the state of New Mexico. There is no longer the denial that students are performing at different levels. Now the question is, "which programs will help us narrow the achievement gap?" (p. 4). The executive summary and full report can be accessed at http://www.abqpartnership.org/.

Chapter 3

1. As presented at NCLB's Web site, http://www.ed.gov/nclb/methods/teachers/ hqtflexibility.html. Highly Qualified Teachers: To be deemed highly qualified, teachers must (1) have a bachelor's degree; (2) have full state certification or licensure; and (3) prove that they know each subject they teach. Under HOUSE, NCLB allows states to develop an additional method for teachers to demonstrate subject-matter competency and meet highly qualified teacher requirements. Proof may consist of a combination of teaching experience, professional development, and knowledge in the subject garnered over time in the profession.

2. Hispanic is used by the U.S. Census Bureau as an inclusive term for any one who speaks Spanish or claims to be of Spanish descent. If one was from Spain this would be accurate, but since speakers of Spanish are from a large number of countries, this explanation is incorrect. Speakers of Spanish languages and descent include, but are not limited to, Latino, Mexican, North American, Mexican-American, Hispano, and Chicano. For further discussion, see the Hispanic Research Institute at the University of New Mexico, http://www.unm.edu/~shri/1/1about_shri.html.

3. In 2005, the Brewster County School District, WC, was sued over Latino discrimination and agreed to send their staff to diversity training; the Boyd Count Public Schools in Kentucky were sued over homosexual discrimination and students were mandated to attend diversity training, which they argued is offensive and demeaning to their religious beliefs.

Chapter 4

1. Cross (1991) reveals the lack of documentation of findings and the connection between group identity and race socialization of African Americans, an aspect of early research that was omitted, which had an impact on the validity of the findings.

2. This is based on W. E. B. Du Bois' theory of duality in the identity of Blacks living near Whites.

3. Schooling, the process of internalizing "the dominant meaning purveyed in formal curricula and school discourse" as presented by Levinson, Foley, and Holland (1996) in *The Cultural Production of the Educated Person* (p. 21), mediates the construction and deconstruction of group and perceived identities during this sensitive stage of early childhood.

4. Critical in this case is referring to discourse grounded in racial realism.

5. Classroom observations were a regular part of my teaching method. These are taken from my kindergarten classes in 1997.

6. Definitions were taken from the top fifteen search results from the *Merriam-Webster Online Dictionary*, http://www.m-w.com/home.htm. Activities to use in classrooms with students focused on critically analyzing dictionary text that have been published at *Rethinking School* and can be found at http://www.rethinkingschools.org.

7. Dr Comer has dedicated his life to the work of the School Development Program in New Haven, CT. His work in removing situational threats from the lives of young children has not only transformed the lives of countless families but of countless White teachers, such as myself, that he so generously gave his time, respect and expertise to for over 30 years.

Chapter 5

1. Children of Color enter school with positive self-perspectives (Holmes, 1995; Porter & Washington, 1989; Spencer, 1999).
2. For a comprehensive discussion on transformative reflection, see hooks (1994, p. 15).
3. Ibid. (p. 14).
4. Ibid. (p.29).

Appendix B

1. Adapted from Kemmis and McTaggart (1988), author permission to reprint.

Appendix C

1. From Strike (1990), author permission to reprint. When discussing equality, I have modified the equality explanation. Strike discusses the need to not make irrelevant judgments based solely on issues of race, gender, etc. But when they are the focus of research and placed within a specific socio-cultural context that then can be held to his standard of equality.

• R E F E R E N C E S •

Aaron, R., & Powell, G. (1982). Feedback practices as a function of teacher and pupil race during reading group instruction. *Journal of Negro Education, 51*, 50-59.

Aboud, F. (1988). *Children and prejudice*. New York: Basil Blackwell.

Aboud, F., & Doyle, A. (1995). The development of in-group pride in Black Canadians. *Journal of Cross-cultural Psychology, 26*(3), 243-254.

Ahlquist, R. (1991). Position and imposition: Power relations in a multicultural foundations class. *Journal of Negro Education, 60*, 158-169.

Allen, R. (2001). The globalization of white supremacy; Toward a critical discourse on the racialization of the world. *Educational Theory, 51*(4), 467-485.

Allen, R. (2002). *Whiteness as territoriality: An analysis of White identity politics in society, education, and theory*. Ann Arbor, MI: ProQuest Information and Learning.

Allen, R. (2005) Whiteness and critical pedagogy. In Z. Leonardo (Ed.), *Critical pedagogy and race* (pp. 53-68). Malden, MA: Blackwell Publishing.

Althusser, L. (1971). *Lenin and Philosophy and Other Essays*. New York and London: Monthly Review Press.

American Renaissance (1990). *Online*, March 2,2008. Retrieved June 30, 2006, from http://www.amren.com/mtnews/archives/2006/03/homeschooling_g.php

Anders, P., & Richardson, V. (1991). Research directions: Staff development that empowers teachers' reflection and enhances instruction. *Language Arts, 68*(4), 316-321.

Anzaldua, G. (1987). *Borderlands/La frontera: The new mestiza*. San Francisco, CA: Aunt Lute Books.

Apple, M. (1996). *Cultural politics and education*. New York: Teachers College Press.

Apple, M. (2000). Official knowledge: Democratic education in a conservative age. New York; London: Routledge.

Apple, M. (2001). *Educating the "right" way: Markets, standards, god, and inequality*. New York: Routledge Falmer.

Asher, S.C., & Allen, V.L. (1969). Racial preference and social comparison processes. *Journal of Social Issues, 25*, 157-165.

Ayvazian, A. (1995). Interrupting the cycle of oppression: The role of allies as agents of change. *Fellowship*, January/February, 6-9.

Baldridge Model of Education. (1987) Retrieved May 5th, 2005 from http://www.baldrigeineducation.org -defunct.

Balibar, E. & Wallerstein, I. (1991). *Race, nation, class: ambiguous identities.* London and New York: Verso Books.

Ballou, D., & Pogursky, M. (1997). *Teacher pay and teacher quality.* Kalamazoo, MI: W.E. Upjohn Institute.

Banks, J. (1994). Multicultural education: Historical development, dimensions, and practice. *Review of Research in Education, 19,* 3-49.

Banks, J. (1993). Approaches to multicultural curriculum reform. In J. Banks & C. Banks (Eds.), *Multicultural education: Issues and perspectives* (2nd ed., 195-214). Boston, MA: Allyn & Bacon.

Banks, J. (1989). Multicultural education: Characteristics and goals. In J. Banks & C. Banks (Eds.), *Multicultural education: issues and perspectives.* Boston: Allyn and Bacon.

Banks, J. (1981). *Education in the 80s: multiethnic education.* Washington, D.C.: National Education Association.

Barba, R., Pang, V., & Tran, M. (1992). Who really discovered aspirin? *The Science Teacher, 59*(5), 26-27.

Bates, K. (2004). Talk about sex: The battles over sex education in the United States. *Journal of the History of Sexuality, 13*(1), 107-110.

Bell, D. (1992). *Faces at the bottom of the well: The permanence of racism.* New York: Basic Books.

Bell, D. (1995). Serving two masters: integration ideals and client interests in school desegregation litigation. In Crenshaw, K. et. al. (Eds.), *Critical race theory: The key writings that formed the movement.* New York: New Press.

Bidol, P. (1971). *Reflections of whiteness in a white racist society* (pamphlet). Detroit: P.A.C.T

Bigelow, B., Christensen, L., Karp, S., Miner, B., & Peterson, B. (1994). *Rethinking our classroom: Teaching for equity and justice an interview with christine sleeter.* Milwaukee, WI: Rethinking Schools.

Billings, G. (1991). Coping with multicultural illiteracy: A teacher education response. *Social Education, 55,* 191-194.

Billings, G., & Henry, A. (1990). Blurring the borders: Voice of African American liberatory pedagogy in the U.S. and Canada. *Journal of Education, 172,* 72-88.

Blair, M. (1998). The myth of neutrality. In P. Connolly & B. Troyna (Eds.), *Researching racism in education, politics, theory and practice* (pp. 16-20). Buckingham, UK; Philadelphia, PA: Open University Press.

Blau, J. (2003). *Race in the schools: perpetuating white dominance?* Lynn Rienner Publishers.

Bonilla-Silva, B. (2005). Introduction: 'Racism" and 'New Racism': The contours of racial dynamics in contemporary America. In Leonardo, Z. (Ed.), *Critical pedagogy and race.* Massachusetts: Blackwell Publishing Ltd.

Bonilla-Silva, B. (2003). *Racism without racists: Color-blind racism and the persistence of racial inequality in the united states.* New York: Rowan and Littlefield Publishers, Inc.

Bonilla-Silva, B. (2001). *White supremacy and racism in the post-civil rights era.* Bolder, Co: Lynn Rienner Publishers.

Bourdieu. P. (1998). *Acts of resistance.* New York: New Press.

Bourdieu, P., & Passeron, J.C. (1977). Reproduction: In education, society, and *culture.* Beverly Hills, CA: Sage.

Britzman, D. (1991). *Practice makes practice: A critical study of learning to teach.* Albany, New York: SUNY Press.

Brophy, J. (1983). Research on the self-fulfilling prophecy and teacher expectations. *Journal of Educational Psychology, 75*, 631-661.

Brophy, J., & Good, T. (1970). Teachers' communication of differential expectations for children's classroom performance. *Journal of Educational Psychology, 61*, 365-374.

Brophy, J., & Good, T. (1986). Teacher behavior and student achievement. In M.C. Wittrock (Ed.), *Handbook of research on teaching* (3rd ed.) (pp. 328-375). New York: Macmillan.

Bruner, J. (1996). *The culture of education.* Cambridge, MA: Harvard University Press.

Burns, R. (1979). *The self-concept: Theory, measurement, development, and behavior.* New York: Longman.

Byrnes, D., & Kiger, G. (1986-1987). Structural correlates of school children's religious intolerance. *Educational Research Quarterly, 11*(3), 18-25.

Carney, C. & Kahn, K. (1984). Building competencies for effective cross-cultural counseling: a developmental view. *The Counseling Psychologist, 12* (1), 111-119.

Casteel, C. (1998). Teacher-student interactions and race in integrated classrooms. *The Journal of Educational Research, 92*(2), 115-120.

Casteel, C. (2000). African american students' perceptions of their treatment by Caucasian teachers. *Journal of Instructional Psychology, 27*(3), 143-148.

Cben, M. (1995). Television as a tool (pp. 1-2). Article based on *Talk with your kids about TV,* The Children & Media Program, Children Now.

Cecil, N. (1988). African American dialect and academic success: a study of teacher expectations. *Reading Improvement, 25*, 34-38.

Children Now. (2003). *Fall colors: Prime-time diversity report.* Oakland and Los Angeles CA.

Children Now. (2000). *Fall colors: How diverse is the prime-time lineup?* Oakland and Los Angeles CA.

Children Now. (2001). *The local television news media's picture of children.* Oakland and Los Angeles CA.

Children Now. (1996). *Television as a tool.* Oakland and Los Angeles CA.

Cochran-Smith, M. (1995). Uncertain allies: Understanding the boundaries of race and teaching. *Harvard Educational Review, 65,* 541-570.

Cohen, D., & Hill, H. (2001). *Learning policy: When state education reform works.* New Haven, CT: Yale University Press.

Cohen, L., Manion, L., & Morrison, K. (2000). *Research methods in education* (5th ed). London: Routledge.

Colby, B. (1991). Coherence theory and metaphor. In J. Fernandez (Ed.), *Beyond metaphor: The theory of tropes in anthropology* (pp. 244-260). Stanford, CA: Stanford University Press.

Coleman, P. & Deutsch, M. (1995). The mediation of inter-ethnic conflict in schools. In W. Hawley and A Jackson (Eds.), *Toward a common destiny: improving race and ethnic relations in america.* San Francisco: Jossey-Bass.

Collins, P. (2000). *Black feminist thought.* (2nd ed.). London: Routledge.

Comer, J., & Poussaint, A. (1992). *Raising black children.* New York: Plume Books.

Comer, J. (1998). Educating poor minority children. *Scientific American* 259(5), 42-48.

Comer, J. (1996). *Rallying the whole village.* New York: Teachers College Press.

Connecticut State Department of Education. (2006). http://www.sde.ct.gov/sde/site/default.asp

Connolly, P. (1998). *Racism, gender identities and young children.* London: Routledge.

Connolly, P., & Neill, J. (2001). Constructions of locality and gender and their impact on the educational aspirations of working class children. *International Studies in Sociology of Education,* 11(2), 107-129.

Connolly, P. (2004). *Boys and schooling in the early years.* London: Routledge Falmer.

Connolly, P. (2003). Gendered and gendering spaces: Playgrounds in the early years. In C. Skelton & B. Francis (Eds.), *Boys and girls in the primary classroom.* Buckingham, UK: Open University Press.

Connolly, P. (1995). Boys will be boys? Racism, sexuality and the construction of masculine identities amongst infant boys. In J. Holland, M. Blair, & S. Sheldon (Eds.), *Debates and issues in feminist research and pedagogy* (pp. 169-

195). Clevedon: Multilingual Matters in Association with the Open University. Reprinted in B. Cosin & M. Hales (Eds.) (1997). *Families, education and social differences* (pp. 164-189). London: Routledge.

Cooper, H., Hinkel, G., & Good, T. (1980). Teachers' beliefs about interaction control and their observed behavioral correlations. *Journal of Educational Psychology, 72,* 345-354.

Corcoran, T., Shields, P., & Zucker, A. (1998). *The SSIs and professional development for teachers.* Menlo Park, CA: SRI International.

Corrigan, P., & Derek, S. (1985). *The great arch: English state formation as cultural revolution.* New York: Basil Blackwell.

Corsaro, W., & Miller, P. (1993). *Interpretive approaches to children's socialization.* San Francisco: Jossey-Bass Inc. Pub.

Corsaro, W., & Rosier, K. (1992). Documenting productive-reproductive processes in children's lives: Transition narratives of a black family living in poverty. *New Directions for Child Development, 58,* 67-91.

Cotton, K. (1993). *Fostering intercultural harmony in schools: Research findings report.* Portland, OR: Northwest Regional Educational Laboratory.

Cotton, K. (1995). *Effective schooling practices: A research synthesis, 1995 update.* Portland, OR: Northwest Regional Educational Laboratory.

Crenshaw, K., Gotanda, N., Peller, G., & Thomas, G. (1995). *Critical race theory: The key writings that formed the movement.* New York: New Press.

Cross, W. (1991). *Shades of black: Diversity in african american identity.* Philadelphia, PA: Temple University Press.

Cross, W. (1985). Black identity: rediscovering the difference between personal identity and reference group orientation. In M. Spencer, G. Brookins, & W. Allen (Eds.), *Beginnings: the social and affective development of black children* (pp. 155-171). New York: Lawrence Erlbaum.

Darling-Hammond, L. (2004). From separate but equal to no child left behind: The collision of new standards and old inequalities. In D. Meier & G. Wood (Eds.), *Many children left behind,* pp 3-32. Boston, MA: Beacon Press.

Darling-Hammond, L. (1997). *Doing what matters most: Investing in quality teaching.* New York: National Commission on Teaching and America's Future.

Davies, B. (1993). *Shards of glass: Children reading and writing beyond gendered identities.* North Sydney, NSW: Allen & Unwin.

Dee, T.S. (2001). *Teachers, race and student achievement in a randomized experiment.* Cambridge, MA: National Bureau of Economic Research.

Delpit, L.D. (1995). *Other people's children: Cultural conflict in the classroom.* New York: New Press.

Derman-Sparks, L. (1989). *Anti-bias curriculum: Tools for empowering young children.* Washington, DC: NAEYC.

Derman-Sparks, L. (1997). *Teaching/learning anti-racism: a developmental approach.* New York: Teachers College Press.

Dewey, J. (1933, 1998). *How we think* (Rev. ed.). Boston, MA: Houghton Mifflin.

Dovidio, J., & Fazio, R. (1992). New technologies for the direct and indirect assessment of attitudes. In J.M. Tanur (Ed.), *Questions about questions* (pp. 204-236). New York: Russell Sage Foundation.

Dovidio, J., & Gaertner, S. (1986). Prejudice, discrimination, and racism: Historical trends and contemporary approaches. In J. Dovidio & S. Gaertner (Eds.), *Prejudice, discrimination, and racism* (pp. 1-34). Orlando, FL: Academic Press.

Doyle, A., Beaudet, J., Aboud, F. (1988). Developmental patterns in the flexibility of children's ethnic attitudes. *Journal of Cross-Cultural Psychology,* 19(1), 3-18.

Du Bois, W. (1903). *The souls of black folk.* Chicago, IL: A.C. McClure & Co.

Dwerk, C. (1975). Role of expectations and attributions in the alleviation of learned helplessness. *Journal of Personality and Social Psychology, 31,* 674-685.

Eagleton, T. (1991). *Ideology: in introduction.* London and New York:Verso.

Earick, M. (2005). *Racial discourse observation protocol.* Early Childhood Racial Identity Equity Self-evaluation Tool. New Mexico: UNM IRB.

Earick, M. (1997). *The white knight.* Unpublished case study. Connecticut.

Elsner, S. (2006). *Home-schooling at home grow in the us.* Rueters. Retrieved March 6, 2006 from http://www.amren.com/mtnews/archives/2006/03/homeschooling_g.php

Fanon, F. (1994). Black skin, white masks. New York: Grove Press.

Fenstermacher, G. (1994). The knower and the known: The nature of knowledge in research on teaching. In L. Darling-Hammond (Ed.), *Review of research in education* (pp. 1-54). Washington, DC: American Educational Research Association.

Fine, M., Weis, L., Powell, C., & Mun Wong, L. (Eds.) (1997). *Off white: readings on race, power and society.* New York: Routledge.

Fisher, C., Berliner, D., Fully, N., Marliave, R., Cahen,L., Dishaw, M. (1980). Teaching behaviors, academic learning time and student achievement: an overview. In C. Denham & A. Lieberman (Eds.), *Time to learn* (pp.7-32). Washington D.C.: National Institute of Education.

Fogg, E. (2006). Conference to promote racism. *Observer Online*, February 17. Retrieved June 30, 2006, from http://observernews.com/stories/current/news/021706/amren.sml

Ford, D. (1985). Self-concept and perception of school atmosphere among urban junior high school students. *Journal of Negro Education, 54*, 74-87.

Foucault, M. (1984/1997). *The Foucault reader.* P. Rainbow (Ed.). New York: Pantheon Books.

Foucault, M. (1971). *Madness and civilization: a history of insanity in the age of reason.* Routledge.

Frankenberg, R. (1993). *White women, race matters: The social construction of Whiteness.* Minneapolis, MN: University of Minnesota Press.

Freire, P. (2000). *Pedagogy of the oppressed.* New York: Continuum International Publishing Group.

Freire, P. (1985). *The politics of education.* New York: Bergin & Garvey Press.

Freire, P. (1970). *Pedagogy of the oppressed.* New York: Continuum International Press.

Gaetner, S. (1976). Nonreactive measures in racial attitude research: a focus on 'liberals". In Katz, P. (Ed.). *Towards the elimination of racism* (pp.183-211). New York: Pergamon Press.

Gage, N. (1978). *The scientific basis of the art of teaching.* New York: Teachers College Press.

Ganter, G. (1977). The socio-conditions of the White practitioner: new perspectives. *Journal of Contemporary Psychotherapy, 9*(1), 26-32.

Garcia, J., Powell, R., & Sanchez, T. (1990). *Multicultural textbooks: How to use them more effectively in the classroom* (ED 320 262). Paper presented at the Annual Meeting of the American Educational Research Association, Boston, MA.

Garet, M., Porter, A., Desimone, L., Birman, B., & Yoon. K. (2001). What makes professional development effective? Results from a national sample of teachers. In *American Educational Research Journal. 38*(4), 915-945.

Gay, G. (2005). Politics of multicultural teacher education. *Journal of Teacher Education, 56*(3), pp. 221-228.

Gay, G., & Howard, T.C. (2001). Multicultural education for the 21st century. *The Teacher Educator, 36*(1), 1-16.

Gay, G. (2000). *Culturally responsive teaching.* New York: Teachers College Press.

Gay, G. (1993). Ethnic minorities and educational equality. In J. Banks & C. Banks (Eds.), *Multicultural education: Issues and perspectives* (2nd ed.) (pp. 171-194). Needham Heights, MA: Allyn & Bacon.

Grant, C., & Secada, W. (1990). Preparing teachers for diversity. In W.R Houston (Ed.). *Handbook on teacher education* (pp. 403-422). New York: Macmillan.

Geuss R. (1981). *The idea of critical literacy.* London: Cambridge University Press.

Gillborn, D., & Mirza, H.S. (2000). *Educational inequality: Mapping race, class and gender.* London: OFSTED.

Gimmestad, B., & DeChiara, E. (1982). Dramatic plays: A vehicle for prejudice reduction in the elementary school. *Journal of Educational Research, 76,* 45-49.

Giroux, H. (2001). *Theory and resistance in education.* Westport, CT: Bergin &Garvey.

Giroux, H. (2000). *Stealing innocence: Corporate culture's war on children.* New York: Palgrave.

Giroux, H. (1997). *Pedagogy and the politics of hope: Theory, culture and schooling.* Boulder, CO: Westview.

Giroux, H. (1995). Series foreword. In J. Jipson, P. Muro, S. Victor, K. Jones, & G. Free Rowland (Eds.), *Reposition feminism and education: Perspectives on education for social change* (ix), CT: Bergin & Garvey.

Giroux, H. (1992). *Border crossing: Cultural workers and the politics of education.* New York: Routledge.

Gitomer, D., Latham, A., & Ziomek, R. (1999). *The academic quality of prospective teacher: The impact of admission and licensure testing.* Princeton, NJ: Educational Testing Service.

Good, T. (1981). Teacher expectations and student perceptions: A decade of research. *Educational Leadership.* 38(5), 415-422.

Good, T., & Grouws, D. (1979). The Missouri mathematics effectiveness project: An experimental study of fourth grade classrooms. *Journal of Educational Psychology, 71*(3), 355-362.

Gramsci, A. (1971). *Selections from the prison notebook.* Q. Hoare & G. Smith (Ed. & Trans.). London: Lawrence & Wishart.

Grossman, P., Wineburg, S., & Woolworth, S. (2001). Toward a theory of teacher community. *Teachers College Record, 103*(6), 942-1012.

Guba, E., & Lincoln, Y. (1994). Competing paradigms in qualitative research. In N. Denzin & Y. Lincoln (Eds.), *Handbook of qualitative research* (pp.105-117). Thousand Oaks: Sage Publications.

Guthrie, E. (1946). Psychological facts and psychological theory. *American Psychological Association, 43*(1), 1-20.

Gutiérrez, K., Baquedano-López, P., & Tejada, C. (1999). Rethinking diversity: Hybridity and hybrid language practices in the third space. *Mind, Culture, and Activity*, 6(4), 286-303.

Gutiérrez, K., Rymes, B., & Larson, J. (1995). Script, counterscript, and underlife in the classroom: James Brown versus Brown v. Board of Education. *Harvard Educational Review*, 65, 445-471.

Haberman, M. (1990). The nature of multicultural teaching and learning in american society. *Peabody Journal of Education*, 65, 101-113.

Hall, S. (1996). Introduction: who needs identity. In Hall, S & duGay, P. (Eds), *Questions of cultural identity* London: Sage.

Hamilton, C., & Carmichael, S. (1967). *Black power: The politics of liberation in America*. New York: Random House.

Hannaway, J., Liu, S., & Nakib, Y. (2003). *Teacher quality: Current status and outlook: The good, the bad and the uncertain.* Paper presented at the meeting of the American Education Finance Association.

Hansell, S. (1981). Teacher race and expectations for student achievement. *American Educational Research Journal*, 18, 191-201.

Hardiman, R. (1982). *White identity development: a process oriented model for describing the racial consciousness of white americans.* ScholarWorks@UMass Amherst.

Hardiman, R. (1979). *White identity development.* Unpublished manuscript.

Harnad, S. (1982). Neoconstructivism: A unifying theme for the cognitive sciences. In T. Simon & R. Scholes (Eds.), *Language, mind and brain* (pp. 1-11). Hillsdale, NJ: Lawrence Erlbaum. Retrieved June 30, 2006, from http://cogsci.soton.ac.uk/~harnad/Papers/Harnad/harnad82.neoconst.html

Harris, C. (1995). Whiteness as property. In K. Crenshaw, N. Gotanda, G. Peller, & K. Thomas, (Eds.), *Critical race theory: key writings that formed a movement*, (pp.276-291). New York: The New Press.

Hart, T., & Lumsden, L. (1989). Confronting racism in the schools. *OSSC Bulletin.*

Harter, S. (1983). Construction perspectives on the self-system. In P. Mussen & E. Hetherington (Eds.), *Handbook of child psychology: Vol. 4. Socialization, personality, and social development* (pp. 275-386). New York: John Wiley.

Harvard University (2002). *Racial inequity in special education, a shocking trend in our nation's public schools.* Retrieved October 9, 2005, from http://www.law.harvard.edu/civilrights/press_releases/special_ed.html

Heaton, R., & Lampert, M. (1993). Learning to hear voices: Inventing a new pedagogy of teacher education. In K.K. Cohen, M.W. McLaughlin, & J.E.

Talbert (Eds.), *Teaching for understanding: Challenges for policy and practice* (pp. 43-83). San Francisco, CA: Jossey-Bass.

Helms, J. (1990, 1993). *Black and white racial identity: Theory, research and practice.* Westport, CT; London: Praeger.

Heppner, M., Multon, K., Gysbers, N., Ellis, C., & Zook, C. (1998). The relationship of trainee self-efficacy to the process and outcome of career counseling. *Journal of Counseling Psychology, 45,* 393-402.

Heppner, P., & Roehlke, H. (1984). Differences among supervisees at different levels of training: Implications for a developmental model of supervision. *Journal of Counseling Psychology, 31,* 76-90.

Hess, F. (2006, May 12). *Tough love for Schools: Essays on competition, accountability, and excellence.* Washington, DC: AEI Press.

Hess, F. (2004). *Retooling K-12 giving.* American Enterprise Institute for Public Policy Research. AEI Print Index No. 17427 (October 7). Retrieved July 1, 2006, from http://www.aei.org/publications/pubID.21345,filter.all/pub_detail.asp

Hillerman, S. & Davenport, G. (1978). Teacher –student interactions in desegregated schools. *Journal of Educational Psychology. 70,* 545-554.

Hodge, J.L., Struckmann, D.K., & Trost, L.D. (1975). *Cultural bases of racism and group oppression.* Berkeley, CA: Two Rider Press.

Hodge, R. & Kress, G. (1988). *Social semiotics,* Ithaca, NY: Cornell University Press.

Holliday, B. (1985). Differential effects of children's self-perceptions and teachers' perceptions on African American children's academic achievement. *Journal of Negro Education, 54,* 71-81.

Holmes, R. (1995). How young children perceive race. *Race and ethnic relations.* Thousand Oaks, CA: Sage.

Honeyford, R. (1986). Anti-racist rhetoric. In F. Palmer (Ed.), *Anti-racism: An assault on education and values (pp.43-60).* London: Sherwood Press.

hooks, b. (1994). *Teaching to transgress: Education as the practice of freedom.* New York: Routledge.

Hopson, D., & Hopson, D. (1990). *Different and wonderful: Raising black children in a race-conscience society.* New York: Simon & Schuster.

Houlgate, S. (Ed.) (1998). *The Hegel reader.* Oxford: Blackwell.

Howard, G. (1999). *We Can'tt Teach What We Don't Know: White Teachers, Multiracial Schools.* New York: Teachers College Press.

Howard, T.C. (2001). Powerful pedagogy for African American students: Conceptions of culturally relevant pedagogy. *Urban Education, 36*(2), 179-202.

Ingersoll, R. (1999). The problem of underqualified teachers in American secondary schools. *Educational Researcher, 28*, 26-36.

Janzen, R. (1994). Five paradigms of ethnic relations. *Social Education, 58*(6), 349-353.

Jeffcoate, R. (1984). *Ethnic minorities and education*. London: Harper & Row.

Johnson, B., & Christensen, L. (2000). *Educational research: Qualitative and quantitative approaches*. London: Allyn & Bacon.

Jones, J. (1981). The concept of racism and its changing reality. In B. Bowser & R. Hunt (Eds.), *Impact of racism on white americans* (pp. 27-49). Beverly Hills, CA: Sage.

Jones, J. (1972). *Prejudice and racism*. Reading, MA: Addison-Wesley.

Kailin, J. (1994). Anti-racist staff development. *Teaching and Teacher Education, 10*, 169-184.

Kailin, J. (2002). *Antiracist education: from theory to practice*. Rowan & Littlefield.

Kailin, J. (1999). How white teachers perceive the problem of racism in their schools: A case study in "liberal" lakeview. *Teachers College Record, 100*(4), 724-750.

Katz, J. (1978). *White awareness handbook for anti-racist training*. Norman: University of Oklahoma Press.

Katz, J. & Ivey, A. (1977). White awareness the frontier of racism awareness training. *Personnel and Guidance Journal, 55*(8), 485-89.

Katz, P.A., & Barrett, M. (1997). *Early predictors of children's intergroup attitudes.* Paper presented at the Annual Meeting of the American Psychological Association (105th, Chicago, IL. August 15-19).

Katz, P.A. (1987). Developmental and social processes in ethnic attitudes ans self-identification. In J. Phinney & M. Rotherham (Eds.), *Children's ethnic socialization: Pluralism and development* (pp. 74-92). London: Sage.

Katz, P. A. & Zalk, S. (1978). Modification of children's racial attitudes. *Developmental Psychology, 14*(5), 447-461.

Kemmis, S., & McTaggart, R. (Eds.) (1992). *The action research planner* (3rd ed.). Geelong Victoria, Australia: Deakin University Press.

Kemmis, S., & McTaggart, R. (Eds.) (1988). *The action research planner* (2nd ed.). Geelong Victoria, Australia: Deakin University Press.

Kemmis, S., & McTaggart, R. (Eds.) (1981). *The action research planner*. Geelong Victoria, Australia: Deakin University Press.

Kincheloe, J. (2003). *Teacher as researcher*. London; New York: Routledge Falmer.

Kincheloe, J. (2002). *The sign of the burger: Mc Donald's and the culture of power*. Philadelphia, PA: Temple University Press.

Kohn, A. (1998). Only for my kid: How privileged parents undermine school reform. *Phi Delta Kappa, 79,* 569-577. Retrieved July 1, 2005, from http://www.alfiekohn.org/teaching/ofmk.htm

Kovel, J. (1970). *White racism: a psychohistory.* New York: Pantheon Books.

Kunjufu, J. (1990). *Countering the conspiracy to destroy black boys.* Chicago, IL: African American Images.

Ladson-Billings, G. (2001b). Racialized discourses and ethnic epistemologies. In N. Denizen & Y.S. Lincoln (Eds.), *Handbook of qualitative research* (pp. 259-277). Thousand Oaks, CA: Sage.

Ladson-Billings, G. (2001a). *Crossing over to Canaan, the journey of new teachers in diverse classrooms.* San Francisco, CA: Jossey-Bass.

Ladson-Billings, G. (2000). Fighting for our lives, preparing teachers to teach african american students. *Journal of Teacher Education, 51*(3), 206-214.

Ladson-Billings, (1995). Towards a theory of culturally relevant pedagogy. *American Education Research Journal, 32,* 465-49.

Ladson-Billings, G. (1994). *The dreamkeepers.* San Francisco, CA: Jossey-Bass.

Lakoff, G. (1987). *Women, fire, and dangerous things: What categories reveal about the mind.* Chicago, IL: University of Chicago Press.

Lakoff, G., & Johnson, M. (1980). *Metaphors we live by.* Chicago, IL; London: University of Chicago Press.

Landsman, J. (2001). *A White teacher talks about race.* Lanham, MD: Scarecrow Press.

Lawrence, S.M., & Tatum, B.D. (1997a). Teachers in transition: The impact of antiracist professional development on classroom practice. *Teachers College Record, 99*(1), 162-178.

Lawrence, S.M., & Tatum, B.D. (1997b). White educators as allies: Moving from awareness to action. In M. Fine, L. Weiss, L. Powell, & M. Wong (Eds.), *Off white: Readings on society, race and culture* (pp. 331-342). New York: Routledge.

Lee, E. (1995). *Letters to Marcia: A teacher's guide to anti-racist education.* Toronto, ON: Cross-cultural Communication Centre.

Leonardo, Z. (2005). *Critical pedagogy and race.* New York: Wiley-Blackwell.

Leonardo, Z. (2003). *Ideology, discourse, and school reform.* New Haven, CT: Praeger.

Levinson, B.A., Foley, D.E., & Holland, D.C. (Eds.) (1996). *The cultural production of the educated person: Critical ethnographies of schooling and local practice.* Albany, NY: State University of New York Press.

Lipman, P. (2004). Education accountability and repression of democracy post-9/11. *Journal for Critical Education Policy Studies, 2*(1), 52-72.

Lipsky, S. (2006). Internalized racism: A major breakthrough has been achieved. *Black Re-emergence, 2.* Retrieved July 20, 2006, from www.rc.org

Loeb, S. (2000). How teachers' choices affect what a dollar can buy: Wages and quality in K-12 schooling. *Education Finance Research Consortium Symposium on the Teaching Workforce.* Albany, NY: University of Albany Center for Policy Research.

Lopez, G. (2001). Revisiting white racism in educational research: Critical race theory and the problem of method. *Educational Researcher, 30*(1), 29-33.

López, H. (1995). The social construction of race. In R. Delgado (Ed.), *Critical race theory: The cutting edge* (pp. 163-175). Philadelphia, PA: Temple University Press.

Lynch, J. (1987). *Prejudice reduction and the schools.* London: Cassell.

Macedo, D. (2000). Introduction. In P. Freire, *Pedagogy of the oppressed* (pp.11-28). New York: Continuum International Publishing Group.

Manning, P. & Cullum-Swan, B. (1994). Narrative, content, and semiotic analyses. In N.K. Denzin & Y. S. Lincoln (Eds.), *Handbook of qualitative research* (pp. 463-478). Thousand Oaks: Sage.

Marcus, G., Gross, S., & Seefeldt, C. (1991). African-american and Caucasian students' perceptions of teacher treatment. *The Journal of Educational Research, 84,*363-367.

Marks, J. (1986). Anti-racism: Revolution not education. In F. Palmer (Ed.), *Antiracism: An assault on education and value* (pp. 32-41). London: Sherwood Press.

Marshall, P. (2002). Racial identity and challenges of educating white youths for cultural diversity. *Multicultural Perspectives, 4*(3), 9-14.

McAdoo, H.P. (1985). Racial attitudes and self-concept of young black children over time. In H.P. McAdoo (Ed.), *Black families* (pp. 213-242). Thousand Oaks, CA: Sage.

McCarthy, S., & Peterson, P. (1993). Creating classroom practice within the context of a restructured professional development school. In K. Cohen, M. McLaughlin, & J. Talbert (Eds.), *Teaching for understanding: Challenges for policy and practice* (pp. 130-166). San Francisco, CA: Jossey-Bass.

McConahay, J. (1986). Modern racism, ambivalence, and the modern racism scale. In J. Dovidio & S. Gaertner (Eds.), *Prejudice, discrimination, and racism* (pp. 1-34). Orlando, FL: Academic Press.

McIntosh, P. (2000). Interactive phases of personal and curricular re-vision with regard to race. In G. Shin & P. Gorski (Eds.), *Multicultural resource series: Professional development for educators.* Washington, DC: National Education Association.

McIntosh, P. (1998). *White privilege and male privilege: A personal account of coming to see correspondences through work in women's studies.* Working Paper 189. Wellesley, MA: Wellesley College Center for Research on Women.

McIntosh, P. (1992) White privilege and male privilege. In M. L Andersen & P.H. Collins (Eds.), *Race, and class and gender.* Belmont, CA:Wadsworth.

McIntosh, P. (1989,1990). *Interactive phases of curricular and personal revision with regard to race.* Working Paper 219. Wellesley. MA: Wellesley College Center for Research on Women.

McIntosh, P. (1988). *White privilege: unpacking the invisible knapsack.* Working Paper 189. Wellesley, MA: Wellesley College Center for Research on Women.

McIntyre, A. (1997). *Making meaning of whiteness: Exploring racial identity with White teachers.* Albany, NY: State University of New York Press.

McLaren, P. (2000). *Che Guevara, Paulo Freire, and the pedagogy of the revolution.* Lanham, MD: Rowman & Littlefield.

Meire, K., Stewart, J., & England, R. (1989). *Race, class and education.* Madison: University of Wisconsin Press.

Melnick, S., & Gomez, M. (Eds.). *Currents of reform in preservice teacher education* (pp. 133-175). New York: Teachers College Press.

Merrick, R. (1988). *Multicultural education: A step toward pluralism* (ED 302 451). South Bend, IN: Indiana University at South Bend.

Mills, C. (1999). *The racial contract.* Ithaca, NY; London: Cornell University Press.

Miner, B., & Peterson, B. (2001). Diversity vs. white privilege. *Rethinking schools online, 15*(2). Retrieved February 20, 2003, from http://www.rethinkingschools.org/archive/15_02/Int152.shtml

Minh-Ha, T. (1989). *Woman, native, other.* Bloomington, IN: Indiana University Press.

Minh-Ha, T. (1996). *Gender and cultural politics.* Paper presented at the National Association of Women in Catholic Higher Education, Boston College, MA.

Moll, L. (1989). Teaching second language students: A Vygotskian perspective. In D. Johnston & D. Roen (Eds.), *Richness in writing: Empowering ESL students,* (pp. 55-69). New York: Longman.

Morrison, T. (1993). *Dancing in the dark: Whiteness and literary imagination.* New York: Vintage.

Murray, C.B., & Jackson, J.S. (1999). The conditioned failure model revisited. In R.L. Jones (Ed.), *African American children, youth, and parenting* (pp.51-81). Hampton, VA: Cobb & Henry.

NAECY (1994). *NAEYC guidelines for preparation of early childhood professionals.* Washington, DC: Author.

National Collaborative on Diversity in the Teaching Force. (2004). *Assessment of diversity in america's teaching force.* Washington, D.C: National Education Association.

NCCP. (2006). *Child poverty.* http://www.nccp.org/topics/childpoverty.html

NCES (2004). *The condition of education 2004* in brief. U.S. Department of Education Institute Sciences: NCES 20004-076.

Nieto, S. (2002). *Language, culture and teaching.* New Jersey & London: Lawrence Erlbaum Associates.

Nieto, S. (2000). *Affirming diversity: The sociopolitical context of multicultural education* (3rd ed.). New York: Longman.

Nieto, S. (1994a). Lessons from students on creating a chance to dream. *Harvard Educational Review,* 64(45), 392-426.

Nieto, S. (1994b). Moving beyond tolerance in multicultural education. *Multicultural Education, 1*(4), 9-12, 35-38.

Northwest Regional Educational Laboratory (NWREL) (1997). *The fourth r; responsibility ensuring educational excellence through equity and effective school practices: An equity handbook for learning communities.* Portland, OR: Center for National Origin, Race and Sex Equity.

Obidah, J. & Teel, M. (2001). *Because of the children: facing racial and cultural differences in schools.* New York: Teachers College Press.

Omi, M., & Winant, H. (1994). *Racial formation in the United States.* New York: Routledge.

Once, M. (1995). Immigrants and education. In J.A. Banks & C.A. McGee Banks (Eds.), *Handbook of research on multicultural education* (pp. 310-327). New York: Simon & Schuster.

Orfield, G., & Eaton, S. (eds.) (1996). *Dismantling desegregation: The quiet reversal of Brown v. Board of Education.* New York: New Press.

Orfield, G. (1995). Schools more separate; Janet Ward Schofield. "Review of Research on School Desegregation's Impact on Elementary and Secondary School Students." In J. Banks & C. Banks (Eds.), *Handbook of research on multicultural education* (pp. 597-617). New York: Simon & Schuster.

Ortiz, M. (2001). *The literacy related beliefs and practices of three primary bilingual teachers.* Tucson, AZ: University of Arizona.

Palincsar, A., Magnusson, S., Marano, N., Ford, D. & Brown, N. (1998). Designing a community of practice: Principles and practices of the GIsML community. *Teaching and Teacher Education,* 14(1), 5-19.

Paley, V. (2000). *White teacher.* Cambridge, MA: Harvard University Press.

Palmer, F. (1986). *Anti-racism: An assault on education and value.* London: Sherwood Press.

Palmer, P.J. (1998). *The courage to teach.* San Francisco, CA: Jossey-Bass.

Pan, B.A., & Snow, C.E. (1999). The development of conversation and discourse. In M. Barrett (Ed.), *The development of language* (pp. 229-250). London: UCL Press.

Patchen, M. (1982). *African american-caucasian contact in schools: Its social and academic effects.* WestLafayette, IN: Purdue University Press.

Pate, G. (1981). Research on prejudice reduction. *Educational Leadership,* January, 288-291.

Pate, G. (1988). Research on reducing prejudice. *Social Education,* April/May, 287-289.

Pavlov, I. (1927). *Conditioned reflexes.* London: Oxford University Press.

Peck, S. (2003). I do have the right. You can't strip it from me: Valuing teachers' knowledge during literacy instructional change. In D.L. Schallert, C.M. Fairbanks, J. Worthy, B. Maloch, & J.V. Hoffman (Eds.), *Fifty-first yearbook of the national reading conference* (pp. 344-356). Oak Creek, WI: National Reading Conference.

Perry, P. (2002). *Shades of white: White kids and racial identities in schools.* Durham, NC: Duke University Press.

Persell, C. (1993). Social class and educational equity. In J. Banks & C. Banks (Eds.), *Multicultural education: Issues and perspectives.* Needham Heights, MA: Allyn & Bacon.

Pettigrew, T., & Meertens, R. (1995). Subtle and blatant prejudice in western europe. *Journal of Social Psychology, 25,* 57-75.

Pettigrew, T. (1981). Race and class in the 1980s: An interactive view. *Daedalus, 110,* 233-55.

Piaget, J.S. (1952). *The child's conception of the world.* London: Routledge & Kegan Paul.

Porter, J. & Washington, R. (1993). Minority identity and self-esteem. *Annual Review of Sociology,* 19, 139-61.

Porter, J. & Washington, R. (1989). *Developments in research on black identity and self* esteem. *Review International Social Psychology,* 2, 3431-53.

Postman, N., & Weingartner, C. (1969). *Teaching as a subversive activity.* New York: Dell.

Quinn, N. (1991). The cultural basis of metaphor. In J. Fernandez (Ed.), *Beyond metaphor: The theory of tropes in anthropology* (pp. 56-94). Stanford, CA: Stanford University Press.

Ramsey, P. (1987). Young children and thinking about ethnic difference. In J. S. Phinney & M. Rotheram (Eds.), *Children's ethnic socialization: pluralism and development*, (pp. 56–72). California: Sage Publications.

Rabinow, K., & Cooper, J. (1981). School's racial mix can affect teacher attitude. *Phi Delta Kappan, 64*, 745-746.

Rethinking Schools Online. http://www.rethinkingschools.org/

Richardson, V. (2003). Constructivist pedagogy. *Teachers College Record, 105*(9), 1623-1640.

Richardson, V., & Anders, P. (2005). Professional preparation and development of teachers. In J. Flood & P. Anders (Eds.), *Literacy development of students in urban schools: Research and policy* (pp. 205-230). Newark, DE: International Reading Association.

Rist, M. (1991). Ethnocentric education. *The American School Board Journal, 178*(1), 26-29, 39.

Rivkin, S., Hanushek, E., & Kain, J. (1998). *Teachers, schools and academic achievement* (NBER Working Paper 6691). Cambridge, MA: National Bureau of Economic Research.

Rizvi, F., & Crowley, V. (1993). Teachers and the contradictions of culturalism. In G.K. Verma (Ed.), *Inequality and teacher education* (pp. 144-164). London: Falmer.

Robinson, S., Robinson, A., & Bickel, F. (1980). Desegregation: A bibliographic review of teacher attitudes and african american students. *Negro Education* Review, 31, 48-59.

Rosenberg, P. (2004) Color blindness in teacher education: an optical delusion (pp. 257-272). In Fine, M., et al. (Eds.), *Off white: readings on power, privilege and resistance*. New York: Routledge.

Sanders, M. (1997). Overcoming obstacles: Academic achievement as a response to racism and discrimination. *Journal of Negro Education, 66*(1), 83-93.

Saussure, F. ([1916] 1983). *Course in general linguistics* (R. Harris. Trans.). London: Duckworth.

Schley, S., & Snow, C.E. (1992). The conversational skills of school-aged children. *Social Development, 1*, 18-35.

Scholes, R. (1982). *Semiotics and interpretation*. New Haven: Yale University Press.

Schon, D. (1995). *The reflective practitioner: How professionals think in action*. London: Arena.

Semaj, L.T. (1985). Afrikananity, cognition, and external self-identity. In M. Spencer, G. Brookins, & W. Allen (Eds.), *Beginnings: The social and affective construction of black children* (pp. 59-72). Hillsdale, NJ: Lawrence Erlbaum.

Shade, B., Kelly, C., & Oberg, M. (1997). *Creating culturally responsive classrooms.* Washington, DC: American Psychological Association.

Shields, A., March, J., & Adelman, M. (1997). *The SSIS impact on classroom practice* (SRI Project 3612). Menlo Park, CA: SRI International.

Simon, R. (1982). *Gramsci's political thought: An introduction.* London: Lawrence & Wishart.

Skinner, B. (1948). 'Superstition' in the pigeon. *Journal of Experimental Psychology, 38,* 168-172.

Sleeter, C. (1992a). *Keepers of the American dream: A study of staff development and multicultural education.* London: Falmer.

Sleeter, C. (1992b). Resisting racial awareness: How teachers understand the social order from their racial, gender and social class locations. *Educational Foundations, 6*(2), 7-32.

Sleeter, C. & Grant, C. (1993). *Making choices for multicultural education: five approaches to race, class and gender* (2nd Ed.). New York: Merrill.

Smith, M.K. (2002). Globalization and the incorporation of education. *Encyclopedia of informal education.* Retrieved March 24, 2004, from www.infed.org/biblio/globalization.htm.

Smylie, M. (1988). Teacher's views of the effectiveness of sources of learning to teach. *The Elementary School Journal, 89*(5), 543-558.

Snow, C.E., & Tabors, P.O. (1993). Language skills that relate to literacy development. In B. Spodek & O. Saracho (eds.), *Yearbook in early childhood education* (pp. 1-20). New York: Teachers College Press.

Snow, C.E. (1990). The development of definitional skill. *Journal of Child Language, 17,* 697-710.

Snyder, T. (Ed.) (1998). *Digest of education statistics, 1998.* Washington, DC: National Center for Education Statistics, U.S. Department of Education.

Solomon, R.P., & Levine-Rasky, C. (1994). *Accommodation and resistance: Educators' responses to multicultural and antiracist education.* Report to the Department of Canadian Heritage. North York, ON: York University.

Solomon, R., & Levine-Rasky, C. (1996). When principle meets practice: Teachers' contradictory responses to antiracist education. *Alberta Journal of Educational Research, 42*(1), 19-33.

Spencer, M. (1999). Social and cultural influences on school adjustment: The application of an identity-focused cultural ecological perspective. *Educational Psychologist, 34*(1), 43-57.

Spencer, M. (1985). Cultural cognition and social cognition as identity factors in black children's personal growth. In M. Spencer, G. Brookins, & W. Allen (Eds.), *Beginnings: The social and affective construction of black children* (pp. 215-230). Hillsdale, NJ: Lawrence Erlbaum.

Spencer, M.B. (1984). Black children's race awareness, racial attitudes, and self-concept. *Journal of Child Psychology and Psychiatry, 25*, 433-441.

Spencer, M.B. (1982). Personal and group identity of black children: An alternative synthesis. *Genetic Psychology Monographs, 183*, 59-84.

Spring, J. (1998). *Education and the rise of the global economy.* Mahwah, NJ: Lawrence Erlbaum.

Stallings, J., Needels, M., & Stayrook, N. (1980). *How to change the process of teaching basic reading skills in secondary schools: Phase II and phase III. Final report, Rev. materials.* Menlo Park, CA: SRI International.

Steele, C. (2003). Stereotype threat and student achievement. In, Perry, T., Steele, C. & Hilliard, A. (Eds.), *Young, gifted and black* (pp. 109-130). Boston, MA: Beacon Press.

Steele, C. (1997). A threat in the air, how stereotypes shape intellectual identity and performance. *American Psychologist, 52*(6), 613-629.

Stevens, G. (1980). Bias in attributions of positive and negative behavior in children by school psychologists, parents, and teachers. *Perceptual and Motor Skills, 50*, 1283-1290.

Stormfront (1980). http://www.stormfront.org

Strike, K. (1990). The ethics of educational evaluation. In J. Millman & L. Darling-Hammond (Eds.), *A new handbook for teacher evaluation* (pp. 356-373). Beverly Hills, CA: Corwin Press.

Strinati, D. (1995). *An introduction to theories of popular culture.* London: Routledge.

Spring, J. (1998). *Education and the rise of the global economy.* Lawrence Erlbaum Associates.

Suárez-Orozco, M. & Páez, M. (2002). *Latinos: remaking america.* Berkeley, CA: University of California Press.

Swain, C. (2003). *Contemporary voices of white nationalism in america.* Cambridge University Press.

Tatum, B.D. (2004). The road to racial equality. *Black Issues in Higher Education, 21*(10), 34.

Tatum, B.D. &Brown, P. (2000). Improving interethnic relations among youth: A school-based project involving educators, parents, and youth. In *Improving intergroup relations among youth: summary of a research workshop.* Forum on Adolescence, Board on Children, Youth, and Families, commission on Behavioral and Social Sciences and Education. Washington, DC: National Academy Press.

Tatum, B.D. (2000a). Examining racial and cultural thinking. *Educational Leadership, 57*(8), 54-57.

Tatum, B.D. (2000b). Group identity: Changing the outsider's perspective. *George Mason University Civil Rights Law Journal, 10*(2), 357-396.

Tatum, B.D. (1994). Teaching white students about racism: The search for white allies and the restoration of hope. *Teachers College Record, 95*(4), 462-476.

Terry, R. (1977). *For whites only.* Grand Rapids, Mich.: Eerdmans.

Texas Freedom Network. (2006). http://www.tfn.org/site/PageServer

Tobin, J. (1997a). The missing discourse of pleasure and desire. In J. Tobin (Ed.), *Making a place for pleasure in early childhood education* (pp. 1-38). New Haven, CT: Yale University Press.

Tobin, J. (1997b). Playing doctor in two cultures: The United States and Ireland. In J. Tobin (Ed.), *Making a place for pleasure in early childhood education* (pp. 119-158). New Haven, CT: Yale University Press.

Tobin, J. (1995). Post-structural research in early childhood education. In J.A. Hatch (Ed.), *Qualitative research in early childhood settings* (pp. 223-243). Westport, CT: Praeger.

Tobin, J., Wu, D., Davidson, D. (1991). *Preschool in three cultures.* New Haven: Yale University Press.

Troyna, B. (1993). *Racism and education: research perspectives.* Buckingham, UK; Philadelphia, PA: Open University Press.

Troyna, B. (1989). A new planet? Tackling racial inequality in all-white schools and colleges. In G.K. Verma (Ed.), *Education for all: A landmark in pluralism* (pp. 175-191). Lewes, UK: Falmer.

U.S. Bureau of the Census (2004). http://www.census.gov/

Valdéz, G. (1996). *Con respecto: Bridging the distances between culturally diverse families and schools.* New York: Teachers College Press.

Van Ausdale, D., & Feagin, J. (2001). *The first r: How children learn race and racism.* London: Rowman & Littlefield.

Vygotsky, L. (1978). *Mind and society: The development of higher mental processes.* Cambridge, MA: Harvard University Press.

Vygotsky, L. (1962,1986). *Thought and language,* Kozulin, A. (Ed.), Cambridge, MA: MIT Press.

Washington, V. (1980). Teachers in integrated classrooms: profiles of attitudes perceptions, and behavior. *The Elementary School Journal, 80,* 192-201.

Watkins, A., & Kurtz, P. (2001). Using solution-focused intervention to address African American male overrepresentation is special education: A case study. *Children & Schools, 23*(4), 223-235.

Weedon, C. (1997). *Feminist practice & poststructuralist theory.* Oxford: Blackwell Publishers.

Weldon, C. (1997). *Feminist practice and poststructuralist theory* (2nd ed). Malden, MA: Blackwell Publishing.

Weinberg, M. (1983). *The search for quality integrated education.* Westport, CT: Greenwood.

Weinstein, R., Marshall, H., Brattesani, K., & Middlestadt, S. (1982). Student perception of differential treatment in open and traditional classrooms. *Journal of Educational Psychology, 74,* 678-692.

Weis, L., Fine, M., Weseen, S., & Wong, M. (2000). Qualitative research, representations, and social responsibilities. In L. Weis & M. Fine (Eds.), *Speed bumps: A student-friendly guide to qualitative research* (pp. 32-66). New York: Teachers College Press.

Werstch, J.V. (1985). *Vygotsky and the social formation of the mind.* Cambridge, MA: Harvard University Press.

Wiley, D., & Yoon, B. (1995). Teacher reports on opportunity to learn: Analyses of the 1993 California learning assessment system (CLAS). *Educational Evaluation and Policy Analysis, 17*(33), 355-370.

Williams, W. (1982). *The state against blacks.* New York: McGraw-Hill.

Wilson, S., & Berne, J. (1999). Teacher learning and the acquisition of professional knowledge: An examination of research on contemporary professional development. In A. Iran-Nejad & P.D. Pearson (Eds.), *Review of research in education, 24,* 173-209. Washington, DC: American Educational Research Association.

Wilson, S., Miller. C., & Yerkes, C. (1993). Deeply rooted change: A tale of teaching adventurously. In K.K. Cohen, M.W. McLaughlin, & J.E. Talbert (Eds.), *Teaching for understanding: Challenges for policy and practice* (pp. 84-129). San Francisco, CA: Jossey-Bass.

Winant, H. (2004). Behind blue eyes: Whiteness and contemporary u.s. racial politics. In M. Fine, L. Weis, L Pruitt & A. Burns, *Off white: Readings on power, privilege and resistance.* New York: Routledge.

Witty, J., & DeBaryshe, B. (1994). Student and teacher perceptions of teachers' communication of performance expectations in the classroom. *Journal of Classroom Interaction, 29*(1), 1-8.

Woman for Aryan Unity. Retrieved June 29, 2004 from http://www.racusa.org/wau/main.html

Wright, M. (1998). *I am chocolate, you are vanilla: Raising healthy Black and biracial children in a race-conscious world.* San Francisco, CA: Jossey-Bass.

Zeichner, K. (1995). Preparing educators for cross-cultural teaching. In W.D. Hawley & A.W. Jackson (eds.), *Toward a common destiny: Improving race and ethnic relations in America* (pp. 397-422). San Francisco, CA: Jossey-Bass.

Zeichner, K. (1996). Issues of pedagogy, knowledge, and teacher preparation. In B. Williams (Ed.), *Closing the achievement gap: A vision for changing beliefs and practices* (pp. 99-114). Alexandria, VA: Association for Supervision and Curriculum Development (ASCD).

Zeichner, K., & Hoeft, K. (1996). Teacher socialization for cultural diversity. In J. Sikula, T. Buttery, & E. Guyton (Eds.), *Handbook of research on teacher education* (2nd ed.) (pp.525-547). New York: Macmillan.

Zhang, D., & Katsiyannis, A. (2002). Minority representation in special education. *Remedial & Special Education, 23*(3), 180.

RETHINKING CHILDHOOD

JOE L. KINCHELOE & GAILE CANNELLA, *General Editors*

A revolution is occurring regarding the study of childhood. Traditional notions of child development are under attack, as are the methods by which children are studied. At the same time, the nature of childhood itself is changing as children gain access to information once reserved for adults only. Technological innovations, media, and electronic information have narrowed the distinction between adults and children, forcing educators to rethink the world of schooling in this new context.

This series of textbooks and monographs encourages scholarship in all of these areas, eliciting critical investigations in developmental psychology, early childhood education, multicultural education, and cultural studies of childhood.

Proposals and manuscripts may be sent to the general editors:

> Joe L. Kincheloe
> c/o Peter Lang Publishing, Inc.
> 29 Broadway, 18th floor
> New York, New York 10006

To order other books in this series, please contact our Customer Service Department at:

> (800) 770-LANG (within the U.S.)
> (212) 647-7706 (outside the U.S.)
> (212) 647-7707 FAX

Or browse online by series at:
> www.peterlang.com